Multimodal Th
Methodology

This concise guide outlines core theoretical and methodological developments of the growing field of Multimodal (Inter)action Analysis.

The volume unpacks the foundational relationship between multimodality and language and the key concepts which underpin the analysis of multimodal action and interaction and the study of multimodal identity. A focused overview of each concept charts its historical development, reviews the essential literature, and outlines its underlying theoretical frameworks and how it links to analytical tools. Norris illustrates the concept in practice via the inclusion of examples and an image-based transcript, table, or graph.

The book provides a succinct overview of the latest research developments in the field of Multimodal (Inter)action Analysis for early career scholars in the field as well as established researchers looking to stay up-to-date on core developments and learn more about a complementary approach to systemic functional and social semiotic frameworks.

Sigrid Norris is Professor of Multimodal (Inter)action and Director of the AUT Multimodal Research Centre at Auckland University of Technology in New Zealand. She is the author of *Analyzing Multimodal Interaction, Identity in (Inter)action*, and *Systematically Working with Multimodal Data*. She also edits extensively with *4 Volumes on Multimodality* in the Routledge Critical Concepts in Linguistics Series as the latest one, and she is the editor of the international journal *Multimodal Communication*.

Multimodal Theory and Methodology

For the Analysis of (Inter)action and Identity

Sigrid Norris

Routledge
Taylor & Francis Group

LONDON AND NEW YORK

First published 2020 by Routledge

2 Park Square, Milton Park, Abingdon, Oxon OX14 4RN
605 Third Avenue, New York, NY 10017

Routledge is an imprint of the Taylor & Francis Group, an informa business

First issued in paperback 2022

Library of Congress Cataloging-in-Publication Data
Names: Norris, Sigrid, 1961– author.
Title: Multimodal theory and methodology: for the analysis of (inter)action and identity / Sigrid Norris.
Description: New York: Routledge, 2020. |
Series: Routledge focus on linguistics | Includes bibliographical references and index.
Identifiers: LCCN 2019051547 |
Subjects: LCSH: Modality (Linguistics) | Interpersonal communication.
Classification: LCC P99.4.M6 N67 2020 | DDC 415/.6—dc23
LC record available at https://lccn.loc.gov/2019051547

ISBN: 978-0-367-36832-6 (hbk)
ISBN: 978-1-03-233694-7 (pbk)
DOI: 10.4324/9780429351600

Typeset in Times New Roman
by codeMantra

To Luke

Contents

Figures

Tables

Acknowledgments

I wish to thank all scholars who have encouraged me to take a moment to look back and bring all of the concepts together in one precise book. As mentioned below, without your encouragement, this book would not exist.

I would like to particularly thank the researchers and visiting scholars at the AUT Multimodal Research Centre at Auckland University of Technology in New Zealand for their constant curiosity, the many fruitful discussions and the wonderful food that we share.

Further, I would like to thank the Freiburg Institute for Advanced Studies (FRIAS), University of Freiburg, Germany and the People Programme (Marie-Curie Actions) of the European Union's Seventh Framework Programme (FP7/2007–2013) under REA grant agreement no. [609305] for making the conception and writing of this book possible.

Preface and General Introduction

This book would probably not exist, if it had not been for so many scholars asking for a book like this and had it not been for my editors at Routledge encouraging me to write it. Frankly, I have been too busy forging ahead, working on the next project, trying to shed light onto human action, interaction and identity production, to look back. However, looking back has been really beneficial, and now I believe that the book will be very useful as a quick guide or a reference. Individual chapters can be used for individual study for researchers or for upper-level courses to either learn or teach some background notions as outlined in Chapter 1; to learn or teach the theoretical and methodological tools to analyze human action and interaction in their complexity as outlined in Chapter 2; or to learn or teach the theoretical and methodological tools that allow the analysis of identity production in actions and interactions, shedding new light on the complexity, as outlined in Chapter 3. The book can also be used as a companion to *Systematically Working with Multimodal Data* (Norris, 2019), where some of the theoretical/analytical tools are only (but differently) touched upon in Chapter 7. Since the tools are discussed here in detail, using the two books in tandem may be good to gain a deeper understanding of the framework. Of course, those interested in identity production may also wish to read *Identity in (Inter)action* (Norris, 2011a), as that book showcases how the framework is used with many examples from an earlier study.

Writing a short-form book has forced me to explain each concept in a most succinct manner. Because of this shortness, examples in this book are only used for explanatory purposes. Some examples are from actual studies, while others are envisioned. Sometimes it was easier and quicker to give an envisioned example to clarify what a conceptual tool can do and how it is used. This is something that we often do in teaching, but it *is* the great difference between this book and all of my other books and articles, which rely on actual studies, ample transcripts and analyses. In Norris (2019) for example, you can even find a website where you can watch the actual videos that are discussed in the book. Such treatment, however, is unfortunately not possible when writing such a precise little book as this one. While on the one hand, not using real examples throughout may be a shortcoming of the book, on the other hand, not using real examples throughout may be an affordance as well since it allowed me to clearly and easily explain what and how the concepts enable the study of complex actions, interactions and identity.

This book sets out to give an overview of theory and analytical tools for multimodal discourse analysis from an action and interaction point of view (Norris, 2004, 2011b, 2013, 2019). This vantage point champions that it is always *action* that we need to focus upon when trying to illuminate multimodal discourse. All action, as is further explicated in the next chapter, is also interaction. In order to always remind ourselves that we begin our analyses with action, that action is always also interaction, and that all interaction is action, we can clearly indicate our focus by using the term (inter)action.

The chapters in this book are written in such a way that they come together, but can also be read as stand-alone chapters. A reader interested in an overall understanding of multimodal (inter)action analysis may first of all be interested in reading Chapter 1. Here, the theory and methodology are positioned within linguistics, and some important concepts such as *attention*, the *mediated action* and *mode* are clarified.

Whereas, a reader who wishes to use the theory and methodology of multimodal (inter)action analysis in order to study multimodal actions and interactions may delve right into Chapter 2. This chapter guides the reader to understand the pieces of the theory and methodology, and offers a quick entry point into actually doing a multimodal (inter) action analysis. The chapter further offers pointers to relevant further readings to quickly gain a deep understanding of the theory and methodology for the analysis of multimodal actions and interactions.

Alternatively, a reader who wishes to use the theory and methodology of multimodal (inter)action analysis in order to study identity may delve right into Chapter 3. This chapter offers the reader a quick entry point into how concepts and analytical tools are used for the analysis of identity in actions and interactions. Here, too, the reader will find pointers to relevant readings that will guide the reader to gain a quick and deep understanding of the theory and methodology for the analysis of multimodal identity.

References

Norris, S. 2004. *Analyzing multimodal interaction: A methodological framework*. London: Routledge.

Norris, S. 2011a. *Identity in (inter)action: Introducing multimodal (inter)action analysis*. Berlin and Boston, MA: deGruyter Mouton.

Norris, S. 2011b. Three hierarchical positions of deictic gesture in relation to spoken language: A multimodal interaction analysis. *Visual Communication* 10(2), 1–19.

Norris, S. 2013. What is a mode? Smell, olfactory perception, and the notion of mode in multimodal mediated theory. *Multimodal Communication* 2(2), 155–169.

Norris, S. 2019. *Systematically working with multimodal data: Research methods in multimodal discourse analysis*. Hoboken, NJ: Wiley Blackwell.

1 Multimodal Theory and Methodology

Background and Definitions

Introduction

This chapter is not only an introduction to multimodal discourse analysis, but more specifically, an introduction to multimodal (inter)action analysis. The chapter is divided into two parts. The first part discusses how multimodality relates to language and outlines how and why multimodal theory and methodology are important for linguistics. The second part goes into some detail in relation to theory and methodology, briefly discussing literature in regard to relevant concepts that are integral to the explicated theory and methodology. The text that follows each textbox of concise information goes into more detail about the concept, adding a longer example and/or a table and/or a graph to illustrate the concept further. Examples, some real and some envisioned, are used throughout merely to enhance comprehension of the analytical tools.

The chapter is brief and can be used as a guide for understanding the theoretical background of how to analyze everyday (inter)action and identity production. The aim of the chapter is to explicate the theoretical and analytical bases of multimodal discourse analysis, or more specifically, multimodal (inter)action analysis.

This chapter clearly explicates five concepts needed for the analysis of actions and interactions, listing for each in a gray textbox:

1 The history of the concept, that is, when and where it was developed and when and where it was first published. Based on this information, the reader can then go to the reference list and find detailed bibliographical information for further reading.
2 The theory that is embedded in the concept.
3 How the concept is used as an analytical tool to analyze data.
4 Brief practical example(s), elucidating the concept.
5 Some analytical capabilities of the concept.

The following text after each textbox of concise information goes into more detail about the concept, adding a longer example and/or a table and/or a graph to illustrate the concept further.

Multimodal (Inter)action Analysis

History

Multimodal (inter)action analysis, a theory and methodology for the analysis of action, interaction and identity, was initially developed in Norris (2002) and first published in Norris (2004a) with a focus on the analysis of actions and interactions. A first publication on identity production is Norris (2005), followed by other writings and a first book outlining the theory and methodology for the study of identity (Norris 2011a).

Theoretical Essence

The essence of the theory is to analyze human action, interaction and identity holistically on micro, meso and macro levels, which are viewed as each consisting of multiple levels. The theory allows one to study not only distinct levels but also the multiplicity of levels.

Methodological Essence

The methodology is built upon a strong theoretical foundation. Clarity of units of analysis and diverse analytical tools allow for consistency of analysis without determining discoveries or findings. Clarity of methodology allows for replicability and therefore reliability.

Multimodality

Actions, interactions and identity are necessarily multimodal. By examining what people do, we realize that all modes together build one coherent system of communication.

Examples

1 The study of face-to-face interactions.
2 The study of online or mixed online and face-to-face interactions.
3 The study of YouTube, music videos, films, etc.

Some Analytical Capabilities

1   Actions, interactions and identity can be analyzed in their complexity. This means that the context of an (inter)action is analyzed as well as the multimodal (inter)action under scrutiny.

2   The multiplicity of (inter)action can be analyzed due to the various analytical tools that allow for such analysis (see below and Chapters 2 and 3 for detail).

3   The fact that social actors in (inter)action do not focus upon the same things, that is, that each social actor produces and experiences a co-produced (inter)action differently, can be analyzed.

As soon as we speak of *multi*modal interaction, we are moving beyond the most theorized and best understood mode, the mode of language. In order to do a multimodal discourse analysis, we use analytical tools that help us to make sense of the multimodal complexity. Of course, analytical tools are not unusual in linguistics. Just think of phonetics, here, we find analytical tools. As an example, we can take a look at the international phonetic alphabet (IPA), or specifically at the vowel chart (Figure 1.1).

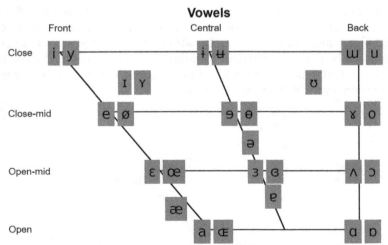

Figure 1.1 Analytical tool: the IPA vowel chart (represented from www. ipachart.com).

This vowel chart is an analytical tool that allows us to place vowels of the world's languages in relation to one another.

With this tool, we can listen to vowels and then place them in relation to the frontness, backness, etc. on the chart. Everyone who has learned to listen to vowels and place them, will, when done correctly, place the same vowel on the chart in an identical place. This tool, the vowel chart, thus allows for reliability and replicability of findings.

But now, let us contemplate syntax as one of our linguistic theories and let us briefly look at Chomsky's universal grammar (Chomsky 1982; Cook and Newson 1996). No matter if we agree with this theory or not, the theory can help us understand an aspect of languages. Just think of a simple sentence such as *The child drew an elephant*. With a universal grammar approach, we can draw a tree diagram and this tree diagram will reflect the grammatical structure of the sentence (Figure 1.2).

Each student who has learned the universal grammar can draw such a tree diagram and, if done correctly, all tree diagrams of this sentence will be identical. Here, the tree diagram is the analytical tool that allows us to understand and portray the underlying structures in sentences.

In both of our examples, in phonetics as well as in syntax, theoretical principles allowed for the development of analytical tools. The analytical tools in turn allow for the analysis of language without determining where vowels of an unknown language would be positioned on the IPA chart, and without predetermining how a tree diagram of a sentence in an unknown language would need to be drawn. Similarly, we find analytical tools in phonology, morphology, semantics and so on, and because of a multitude of analytical tools, we can systematically analyze languages. Similarly, we find analytical tools in discourse analytical approaches. Just think of the turn at talk in conversation analysis (Sacks et al. 1974).

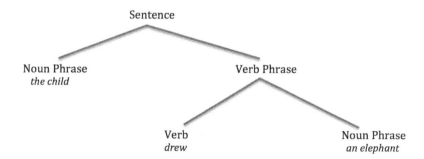

Figure 1.2 Analytical tool: a tree diagram (replicated from Cook and Newson 1996: 4).

Each time a new branch of linguistics was developed, new theories were created and new analytical tools were devised. Similarly, when we moved beyond the study of language in interaction, a new theory was needed and new analytical tools had to be devised. Of course, just as the universal grammar was not developed based on the theoretical foundations or the analytical tools of the international phonetic alphabet, so the theory of multimodal (inter)action is not based on the theoretical foundation of spoken or written language. Rather, language, while being the most researched and well-understood mode, here becomes a (very important) part within the multimodal constellations when people act and interact, illuminating language from a new perspective, allowing us to gain new insight into linguistics.

(Inter)action

History

Beginning of the development in Norris (2002) with a first publication in Norris (2004a), where, however, the term "interaction" was still used in its more common understanding, further developed and clearly stated as (inter)action in Norris (2011a).

Theoretical Essence

(Inter)action is defined as social actor(s) acting or interacting with others, the environment and/or objects.

Methodological Essence

One person can (inter)act alone *or* multiple social actors may (inter)act together.

Examples

1 Peter *plays a computer game.*
2 Laura and Peter *play a card game together.*
3 Mary has a *meeting with several of her coworkers.*

Some Analytical Capabilities

1 Discovery of how a single individual (inter)acts with the environment and objects.
2 Discovery of how two or multiple people simultaneously (inter)act with each other, the environment and objects.

When speaking of (inter)action, we always take human action and interaction as our point of interest. With this, we are neither specifically interested in one or another mode. Yet, with this new vantage point from which we analyze human action and interaction, we are bound to discover new aspects of each mode, *including new aspects of the mode of language*. In Norris (2011a), I explain:

> ...I deviate from the commonly used term *interaction*, calling it here *(inter)action*, instead. With the term *(inter)action*, I broaden the commonly used notion of *interaction*: (inter)action potentially encompasses each and every action that an individual produces with tools, the environment, and other individuals.
>
> (Norris 2011a: 1, italics original)

Examining (inter)action in its complexity and conceiving the multiple modes that people use in action and interaction as one system of communication allows us to look at language through a new lens. Thus, by taking a different angle in the study of human (inter)action, we do gain new insights into the (best understood) mode of language at the same time as we gain new insight into less well-understood modes such as posture, gaze, music or object handling. However, we never just focus upon one or two modes at a time, but always focus upon the *actions* and *interactions* at hand. Actions and interactions are always produced through the coming together of multiple modes, and which ones are more relevant in and for an action or interaction can only be determined through analysis. Thus, as analysts we do not *decide* which modes we will pay particular attention to at the outset. Rather, we may *discover* that some modes are more important in an (inter)action than others.

Thus, as soon as we speak of multimodal (inter)action, *we do not integrate other modes with the study of language* but move beyond the thus far more typical study of language since *we think beyond language*. Such thinking from a vantage point beyond language not only brings with it the ability to theorize multimodal (inter)action in a coherent manner, but it also allows us to take a *different look at language* (and other modes) in (inter)action. In this way, the study of language has not lost its worth; rather, *the study of language has been expanded*, thereby allowing us to shed new insight on areas of language use that have thus far been disregarded or even misunderstood because the vantage point has been too narrow when studying (inter)action.

But it is not only language use that is being considered from a broader vantage point by integrating the multiplicity of all modes in (inter) action. Rather, the term (inter)action itself has been extended in the process of development of this new theory and analytical framework, as is indicated by the parentheses around *inter* to illustrate the difference to earlier definitions of interaction, or indicated by the use of *action and interaction or (inter)actions* as expressing the same notions (Norris 2019). Here, the term (inter)action is defined as social actor(s) (inter)acting with others, the environment and/or objects. Thus, in this theory, one person can interact with a computer, just as two people can interact when having a conversation, or multiple people can (inter)act in a classroom together. However, the computer, other than in actor network theory (Latour 1994, 1996, 2005), always remains a mediational means/cultural tool. In the theory outlined in this book, social actors are people.[1]

(Inter)actional Attention

History

Developed in Norris (2002); first published in Norris, (2004a,b), (inter)actional attention (with parenthesis around *inter*) first used here.

Theoretical Essence

First, the speaker model [where the speaker indicates to the interlocutor what the speaker is focused upon (Chafe 1994; Bard et al. 2000; Arnold and Lao 2015)] is merged with the cooperative speaker model [where the speaker assumes what the interlocutor is focused upon (Clark and Marshall 1981; Levelt 1989; Gundel et al. 1993; Brennan 1995; Bard et al. 2000)]. Second, the concept of (inter)actional attention moves beyond focused attention to a foreground–background continuum of attention/awareness.

Methodological Essence

A graph is used as a heuristic, where the x-axis builds the foreground–background continuum of attention/awareness and the y-axis demonstrates the modal density used by a social actor to produce a specific action (see Chapter 2 for more detail).

Researchers can plot the simultaneously performed actions on this graph to show how the actions are produced relationally to one another.

Examples

1   Peter *plays a computer game and watches a movie.*
2   Laura and Peter *play a card game together and their father is making dinner in the open plan kitchen.*
3   Mary has a *meeting with several of her coworkers, she is (inter) acting with her partner via text messaging and she is checking her emails as she is waiting for a friend to contact her.*

Some Analytical Capabilities

1   Discovery of how attention and awareness levels vary in (inter)actions.
2   Discovery of how social actors co-producing an (inter) action pay different (or the same) focused attention to the (inter)action.

Focused Attention: Some Background

For many discourse analysts, focused interaction is usually unquestionably assumed when the participants use language to communicate. In linguistics, we are interested in the focus of a sentence, a topic, a paragraph or an utterance. In this way, particular interest is paid to referring expressions as they tell us where the speaker thinks the hearer's attention state is at a particular moment. Gundel et al. (1993), for example, explain:

> It is widely recognized that the form of referring expressions... depends on the assumed cognitive status of the referent, i.e. on assumptions that a cooperative speaker can reasonably make regarding the addressee's knowledge and attention state...
>
> (Gundel et al. 1993: 275)

Gundel et al. (1993) here (possibly inadvertently) parrot Levelt (1989) who had made the point while discussing assigning accessibility status to referents:

> What matters here is the estimated *accessibility* of the referent for the addressee ("estimated" because it is the speaker's judgment that matters, not the real accessibility as experienced by the addressee).
>
> (Levelt 1989: 145)

Based on this assumption, Gundel et al. (1993: 279) examine the cognitive status and form of referring expressions in discourse and make the

point that a referent is in focus when it is "at the current center of attention. This status is necessary for appropriate use of zero and unstressed
pronominals." Thus, they show in their work that speakers produce pronominals based on the speaker assessment of hearer knowledge and,
most notably here, based on the speaker assessment of hearer attention.

What Gundel et al. (1993) refer to as "widely recognized" above is
a theoretical assumption that entails "speakers' models of listeners'
knowledge" (Bard et al. 2000: 3). Brennan (1995: 140), working with
this same assumption, explains that "a speaker signals her center of attention by her linguistic choices" and proposes that "such choices help
an addressee track changes in the focus of attention...in a discourse
context." This is not very different from the audience design model
proposed by Bell (1984), where he suggests that speakers shift their
style in relation to the speaker's audience.

Arnold and Lao (2015: 833), however, note that while "[t]he linguistic
context has been proposed to define what is in focus, and what is not...
the causal relationship between discourse focus and attention is unclear."
Examining pronoun comprehension, Arnold and Lao (2015) attempt to
assess the psychological role of attention through eye-tracking and the
assessment of what they call "private attentional fluctuations." Their notions of attention are directed to individual attention, rather than shared
attention. Their view of attention thus differs from Gundel et al. (1993)
and others (Clark and Marshall 1981; Levelt 1989; Brennan 1995).

Gundel et al. (1993: 275) assert that an assumed cognitive status of
discourse entities rests on the "assumptions that a cooperative speaker
can reasonably make regarding the addressee's knowledge and attention state..." Arnold and Lao (2015: 834), however, criticize Gundel
et al. and others because their "approach suggests that reference
processing is only affected by evidence about the attention of one's
interlocutor." Therefore, while many discourse analysts take the cooperative speaker model for granted and see it as a given, others such as
Arnold and Lao (2015) and Bard et al. (2000) oppose this model. As an
example, Bard et al. (2000) demonstrated in their work that speakers
more often than not focus on their own speech production rather than
on a perceived hearer's knowledge or attention state. Similarly, Chafe
(1994: 29) speaks of intonation units and claims that these units are

> ...that part of the speaker's model of reality on which his or her con-
> sciousness is focused at the moment. In a socially interactive situa-
> tion it is the portion on which the speaker intends that the listener's
> consciousness be focused as a result of hearing the intonation unit.
> (Chafe 1994: 29)

Thus, Chafe takes the point of view of the speaker and speaker intention, rather than using the cooperative speaker model. Chafe (1994: 29) goes on to propose that "[t]he active focus is surrounded by a periphery of *semiactive* information that provides a context for it." Chafe (1994) thus goes beyond the active focus and includes a *semiactive periphery* in his understanding of focus in a social interactive situation. As the speaker expresses their focus and semiactive periphery within the intonation units, the hearer's consciousness is focused in order to attain mutual understanding. However, Clark and Marshall (1981: 38) make the point that physical co-presence is "the strongest evidence for mutual knowledge that people are generally prepared to accept." They illustrate their point with two people and a candle, where one of them is referring to the candle. While Clark and Marshall are primarily interested in terms of reference, they do also speak of visual focus when they, for example, explain: "When Ann and Bob are actually focusing on the candle as she says *this candle*, we have a case of *immediate physical copresence*." Here, the physical co-presence is between Ann, Bob and the candle. Immediate physical co-presence thus relies heavily on visual attention.

Many researchers (see Wu, 2014 for a detailed discussion of some of this attention literature) as Wu (2011) discuss the notion of attention as primarily, though not only, visual.

> The synchronic salience of the object to the subject is constituted by this demonstrative representation of that and only that object at a time. What is salient is what one voluntarily maintains attention to and thereby demonstratively represents in being aware of one's so attending.
>
> (Wu 2011: 101)

When thinking about Clark and Marshall's (1981) insistence on the importance of visual co-presence, we can read the description by Wu in relation to the example where Ann speaks with Bob about the candle, all three of them being co-present.

> In response to voluntarily attending to a specific object, the subject actively thinks about it as opposed to other objects perceived, makes plans or deliberates about it as opposed to others, is aware of moving towards and acting on it rather than others and so on. We can say that the attended object also anchors such broadly cognitive activity. One is in general then aware of what one is variously doing, activities that are united by a common anchor: the attended object.
>
> (Wu 2011: 111)

When reading the above excerpt, we also have to realize that attention is selective. In psychology, one often speaks of rejecting stimuli when discussing selective attention. Cherry (1953), in his classic work, reported on findings of selective attention for language understanding. Participants were given different auditory input in each ear and were asked to repeat what they heard from one source. As a result, Cherry could show that the participants rejected the stimuli that streamed into one ear, and as a result, they were unable to say much about this auditory stream. But just as attention can be selective, Helmholz (1896) already demonstrated that attention may be covert, which means that a person can focus their gaze upon one thing, while actually visually attending to something else. Of course, such covert attention is not limited to visual attention. As we all know, students in a class may, for example, demonstrate overt attentive awareness to what a teacher is saying, while they are in fact covertly day-dreaming and are far from paying focused attention to the teaching moment.

But Wu (2014) makes another important point when discussing the epistemic role of attention, where he discusses the emotional, physical, and psychological states of attention.

> My introspection of my pain state that leads to my belief that I am in pain seems to put me in an epistemically privileged position vis-à-vis my pain, as opposed to your belief that I am in pain formed on the basis of your observation of my behavior.
>
> (Wu 2014: 254)

We see that there are many ways of looking at attention, and I would like to make the point that all of these ways of looking at attention are valid and not one of them is more important than another. Yet, the notion of attention is not exhausted as described thus far. Rather, there is another very important way to look at attention that has not been addressed by any of the above quickly summarized research directions, and that is the notion of *(inter)actional attention.*

(Inter)actional Attention: Importance for Discourse Analysts

(Inter)actional attention is particularly important for discourse analysts. The below excerpt summarizes what multimodal (inter)action analysis, the framework in which (inter)actional attention has been proposed, is concerned with.

> In interactional multimodal analysis…we are concerned with the perceptions, thoughts, and feelings that people are expressing. We

can surmise that some perceptions, thoughts, and feelings that are expressed by someone are also somewhat experienced by that person, even though the actual experience and the expression of the experience should not be viewed as a one-to-one representation and may be as diverse as to contradict each other. We can also surmise that not every perception, thought, and feeling that a person experiences is expressed.

(Norris 2004a: 3–4)

There I propose the notion of (inter)actional attention, which is the kind of attention that interlocutors read off of the verbal and nonverbal actions that a person performs. Person A thus performs particular actions, which are in some ways the expressions of what person A experiences, perceives, thinks and feels. Person B then reads these actions performed by person A as the expressions of what person A experiences, perceives, thinks and feels. Person B in turn performs particular actions in relation to how they perceive person A's performed actions.

Thus, here we find that the speaker model where the speaker indicates to the interlocutor what the speaker is focused upon (Chafe 1994; Bard et al. 2000; Arnold and Lao 2015) is merged with the cooperative speaker model where the speaker assumes what the interlocutor is focused upon (Clark and Marshall 1981; Levelt 1989; Gundel et al. 1993; Brennan 1995; Bard et al. 2000). However, here we are not only interested in focused attention.

Modal Density Foreground–Background Continuum of Attention/Awareness

Not entirely unlike Goffman (1974), who had proposed an unattended track of attention or Chafe (1994) who spoke of a semiactive periphery of attention, I (Norris 2004a) suggest that there is more than only focused attention. In fact, I propose a continuum of attention. Further, and unlike both Goffman and Chafe, I suggest that the entire continuum of attention needs to be considered when studying social interaction. Therefore, I suggest that attention and awareness (here taken to be two different sides of the same concept) are analyzable on a foreground–background continuum where the foreground presents focused attention and the background is that level that a performer pays least attention to and/or is least aware of. In order to truly understand when and how social actors focus upon the same interaction, the attention levels of each person need to be analyzed.

In order to analyze the differentiated interactive attention levels that interlocutors engage in, I developed the methodological tool called the *modal density foreground–background continuum of attention/aware-ness*. This analytical tool allows us to analyze interactive attention in great detail and then relationally illustrate particular attentional states on a graph.

Attention: Connecting the Dots

Linguists are strongly interested in the cooperative speaker model (Clark and Marshall 1981; Levelt 1989; Gundel et al. 1993; Brennan 1995) or in the speaker model (Bard et al. 2000; Arnold and Lao 2015) of attention. Psychologists (Pashler 1998) are primarily interested in mechanisms and processes of attention. Whereas multimodal (inter) action analysts combine all of these interests and concentrate upon the *overt multimodal display of attention by one interlocutor and the pro-duced multimodal reaction by another interlocutor*, which in other work (Norris 2002, 2004a, b, 2006, 2008, 2011a, 2016, 2017) has been shown to be a part of a phenomenal conception of attention.

Certainly, a phenomenal conception of attention in itself is not new. James (1890) was already interested in the subjectivity of attention. Fast-forwarding, but still following in James' footsteps, Carrasco et al. (2002, 2004), Gobell and Carrasco (2005), Carrasco (2006) or Tse (2005), for example, showed that a change in focused visual attention can have an effect upon the perception of shapes, color or the size of an object. James, Carrasco and others thus are also interested in the phenomenal conception of attention. However, while James was quite broad in his view of attention, Carrasco and others are particularly in-terested in visual attention. Further, Helmholz, James, Carrasco and others' interest lies in the *attention-perception by the performer* of an action or task. Whereas multimodal (inter)action analysts are inter-ested in the perception of the *attention displayed by the performer of an action and perceived and reacted to by others*. In order to exemplify the point of difference, we can say that Helmholz, James, Carrasco, Carrasco et al. or Tse are interested in *how a student perceives* a teach-ing moment or their day-dreaming, while multimodal (inter)action an-alysts would be interested in *how the student displays their perception of a teaching moment or their day-dreaming, how the teacher perceives the displayed interactive attention of the student and how the teacher reacts to it*. Here, we would ask: 1. What kind of actions does the student perform? What (inter)actional attention can the teacher (or others) read off of these actions? (i.e. Does the student pay more attentional focus to the teaching moment or to day-dreaming)? and How does the teacher react to these portrayed attentional states by the student? (and from there: How does the student respond to the teacher's reaction? and so on, realizing the processes of communication through (inter) actional attention). In order to analyze these questions in a theoretically founded manner, multimodal (inter)action analysis builds upon mediated discourse theory (Scollon 1998, 2001a).

Mediation: Allowing for Integration of History, Memory and Context

Multimodal (inter)action analysis particularly grew out of Scollon's (1997, 1998, 2001a,b) mediated discourse analysis, Wodak's (1989, 1995, 2001) discourse historical approach, interactional sociolinguistics (Goffman 1974; Gumperz 1982; Tannen 1984; Tannen and Wallat 1993), sociocultural psychology (Wertsch 1998) and early parts of social semiotics (Kress and Van Leeuwen 1996, 2001; Van Leeuwen 1999).

With this theoretical background, multimodal (inter)action analysis is an analytical approach to discourse that integrates history, memory and the overall context, allowing for an analysis from the micro- to the meso- and a macro level. One overarching notion that allows for a congruent analysis is the notion of mediation.

Mediation, a theoretical notion first introduced by the sociocultural psychologist Vygotsky (1978), was somewhat redefined by the sociocultural psychologist Wertsch (1998) and further developed by the anthropological linguist Scollon (1998). In multimodal (inter)action analysis, Wertsch's (1998) and Scollon's (1998) notion of "mediated action" and in particular Scollon's (1998) notion of "mediation" is used. Scollon emphasized that all actions are mediated actions and that all actions are always mediated in multiple ways. A mediated action is defined as a social actor acting with or through meditational means or cultural tools (Scollon 1998; Wertsch 1998).

While there is not enough space in this brief introduction to go deeply into this theoretical background, it is important to note that the linguist Scollon (1998, 2001a) claimed that the unit of analysis for discourse analysts needed to be the mediated action rather than the utterance, turn, phrase or text. The mediated action, Scollon assured, always occurs at a site of engagement, which is delineated as the window opened up by converging practices that make a particular concrete mediated action possible. Practices, in Scollon's work, are delineated as mediated actions with a history. Thus, Scollon always emphasized the concrete instantiation of mediated actions in everyday life. He demonstrated that it is the concrete mediated actions that allow a child to learn not only the action (such as handing something to a caregiver), which differs each time depending upon the object that is being handed as well as the social actor that it is handed to, but to simultaneously learn the practice [here, the practice of handing (anything to anybody)]. While Scollon emphasized the mediated action and the converging practices in everyday interaction, his main concern nevertheless remained the use of language in interaction. His primary interest was how and in what way language featured in everyday interaction. However, his theoretical position was always that social actors first of all produce mediated actions, that is, *social actors are doing something*. This doing something, Scollon claimed, could include language but was not limited to using language. Handing something to someone, he suggested, was just as much of a mediated action as was telling somebody something. Whereas handing was mediated by the hand, the arm, the object, the gaze, etc., telling somebody something was mediated by vocal folds, lips, larynx, the language itself and so on. Scollon made the point that each time a mediated action unfolds, the action is mediated in multiple ways, and language is but one cultural tool that can mediate an action. Thus, Scollon (1998, 2001) shifted linguistic inquiry toward the mediated action. Mediation, he asserted, was the theoretical notion that allowed linguists to dig deeper in order to theoretically understand how actions are mediated and when and how language became one of the cultural tools mediating the actions.

It was no big jump from Scollon's mediated discourse theory to a multimodal mediated discourse theory (Norris 2004a, 2013, 2019) because Scollon had already laid the foundation that allowed for linguists to examine mediated actions rather than talk in interaction. With the theoretical notion of the mediated action, theorization of units of analysis became possible, which built upon earlier work in linguistics without, however, being limited by a purely linguistic theory. However, analyzing multiple modes such as gesture, posture, music, layout and gaze as well as language necessitated a theoretical foundation that could deal with the structural as well as physical differences of the various modes (Norris 2004a). A theory building upon Scollon's mediated discourse theory allowed for the development of a new theory that was built purely for the analysis of multimodal (inter)action (Norris 2004a, 2011a, 2013, 2019) in which all modes, no matter their physical or structural makeup could be theorized and analyzed in a cohesive manner. This theory utilized Scollon's theoretical position of the mediated action. First, in Norris (2002, 2004a), I differentiated between several levels of mediated actions and later, in Norris (2013), I defined a mode as a system of mediated action (further explained below). With this definition of a mode, the concept *mode* includes a sociocultural psychological facet, a historical facet as well as an embodied physical facet. Thus, rather than viewing a mode as a resource that social actors can use in order to interact and communicate, the definition of mode as a system of mediated action is strongly theorized to incorporate embodiment, perception, emotion, thought and memory as well as the broader history of actions, interactions and objects.

Mode

History

Problematized since Norris (2002); but first redefined and published as *A mode = System of mediated action with regularities* in Norris (2013).

Theoretical Essence

Defining a mode as a system of (lower-level) mediated actions with regularities:

1   Embraces the *social actor + (always multiple) mediational means* as unit.
2   Allows for the analysis of regularities residing either (more) in the social actor(s) or (more) in the various mediational means.
3   Embraces individual, sociocultural *and* historical characteristics, always keeping the tension between social actor(s) and mediational means alive.
4   Emphasizes that systems of mediated actions are learned in and through (inter)action.
5   Emphasizes that modes are "only" theoretical concepts: We study concrete actions and interactions, but can use this theoretical notion as an abstract way to speak about them.
6   Emphasizes that no one system of mediated action can ever be learned alone, that is, modes in (inter)action are always multiple.

Methodological Essence

Modes (systems of mediated actions are made up of and produce concrete lower-level mediated actions performed by social actors) build an integral part of analytical tools such as the modal density foreground–background continuum of attention/awareness, modal configurations or modal aggregates. Thus, when investigating concrete actions, we can examine them in light of modal makeup.

Examples

1 Peter plays a computer game and watches a movie:
   When Peter pays more attention to one of these (inter)actions, *modal density* is higher for this one than for the other one.
2 Laura and Peter play a card game together and their father is making dinner in the open plan kitchen:
   As the father is making dinner, he also pays attention to the children. Each one of these (inter)actions is made up of different *modal configurations*.
3 Mary has a meeting with several of her coworkers and she is (inter)acting with her partner via text messaging:
   When Mary is texting with her partner, gaze, mobile phone use, object handling and text build a *modal aggregate*.

Some Analytical Capabilities

1 Modal density allows us to discover when and how social actors pay more attention/are more aware of an (inter)action than another.
2 Modal configurations allow us to discover how specific (inter)actions are multimodally produced and how various hierarchical ordering of modes is organized.
3 Modal aggregates allow us to determine which concrete lower-level actions and chains thereof have to be tightly interlinked to make a particular action possible.

Modes are purely heuristic units, defined as systems of mediated action with regularities. These systems of mediated action are learned in and through (inter)action with other social actors, with the environment and with objects. In some sense, we all have acquired modes (or systems of mediated action) differently, yet, in another sense, our acquisition of all modes (or systems of mediated action) overlap with those of others. A mode is simultaneously social, cultural, historical and with this also particular to social actors as they have acquired them in and through their experiences.

The reason we want to think of regularities is that one mode (or system of mediated action) distinguishes itself from another. For example, the mode of walking distinguishes itself from the mode of running. Exactly how one is distinguishable from the other can be found in the regularities that exist in each. However, a distinction between walking and running is not always needed and a larger distinction may be more valuable for the analysis of a particular (inter)action at hand. Thus, when investigating how city-dwellers get to work, we may want to distinguish between moving on foot as a mode and compare this with riding a bicycle as a mode or driving a car as a mode. Moving on foot from point A to point B proceeds in the form of a chain of lower-level mediated action (setting one foot in front of the other). Attached to this mode are certain regularities. Riding a bicycle from point A to point B again proceeds in the form of a chains of lower-level mediated actions (such as peddling); and again, certain regularities can be found in this mode. Similarly, we can speak of driving in this way. But when we come to riding a bicycle or driving, we quickly question which ones of the chains of actions we shall focus on, and the answer is all of them. As illustrated again and again (see, for example, Norris 2004a, 2011a,b, 2013), one mode never is used alone in (inter) action. Modes always come together, they can be defined in various ways (i.e., moving on foot can be defined as a mode or walking can be defined as a mode), and with this framework, we can tease them apart and make sense of multimodal (inter)action.

Conclusion

I end this brief introductory chapter, in which I explicated the overarching notions of the framework, outlining multimodal (inter) action analysis, (inter)action, (inter)actional attention, mediation and mode.

Next, Chapter 2 gives an overview of theoretical concepts and analytical tools for the analysis of multimodal (inter)actions, and Chapter 3 gives an overview of how concepts and tools discussed are used for the study of identity. Both Chapters 2 and 3 build upon the notions discussed in Chapter 1, but each can also be read as a stand-alone chapter.

Note

1 For exceptions from people as social actors, see Norris (2019).

References

Arnold, J.E. and Lao, S.Y.C. 2015. Effects of psychological attention on pronoun comprehension. *Language, Cognition and Neuroscience* 30, 832–852. doi:10.1080/23273798.2015.1017511

Bard, E.G., Anderson, A.H., Sotillo, C., Aylett, M., Doherty- Sneddon, G., and Newlands, A. 2000. Controlling the intelligibility of referring expressions in dialogue. *Journal of Memory and Language* 42(1), 1–22. doi:10.1006/jmla. 1999.2667

Bell, A. 1984. Language style as audience design. In: Coupland, N. and Jaworski, A. (1997, eds.) *Sociolinguistics: A reader and coursebook.* New York: St Martin's Press, 240–250.

Brennan, S.E. 1995. Centering attention in discourse. *Language and Cognitive Processes* 10(2), 137–167. doi:10.1080/01690969508407091

Carrasco, M. 2006. Covert attention increases contrast sensitivity: Psychophycial, neurophysical and neuroimiging studies. *Progress in Brain Research* 154, 33–70.

Carrasco, M., Ling, S., and Read, S. 2004. Attention alters appearance. *Nature Neuroscience* 7(3), 308–313.

Carrasco, M., William P.E., and Yeshurun, Y. 2002. Covert attention increases spatial resolution with or without masks: Support for signal enhancement. *Journal of Vision* 2(6), 467–479.

Chafe, W. 1994. Prosodic and functional units of language. In: Edwards, J. and Lampert, M. (eds.) *Talking data: Transcription and coding in discourse research.* Hillsdale, NJ: Lawrence Erlbaum Associates, 3–31.

Cherry, E.C. 1953. Some experiments on the recognition of speech, with one and with two ears. *Journal of the Acoustic Society of America* 25, 975–979.

Chomsky, N. 1982. *Some concepts and consequences of the theory of government and binding.* Cambridge, MA: MIT Press.

Clark, H.H. and Marshall, C.R. 1981. Definite reference and mutual knowledge. In: Joshi, A.K., Webber, B.L., and Sag, I.A. (eds.) *Elements of discourse understanding.* Cambridge: Cambridge University Press, 10–63.

Cook, V.J. and Newson, M. 1996. *Chomsky's universal grammar: An introduction.* Cambridge, MA: Blackwell.

Gobell, J. and Carrasco, M. 2005. Attention alters the appearance of spatial frequency and gap size. *Psychological Science* 16(8), 644–651.

Goffman, E. 1974. *Frame analysis.* New York: Harper & Row.

Gumperz, J. 1982. *Discourse strategies.* Cambridge: Cambridge University.

Gundel, J.K., Hedberg, N., and Zacharski, R. (1993). Cognitive status and the form of referring expressions in discourse. *Language* 69, 274–307. doi:10.2307/416535

Helmholz, Hermann von. 1896. *Handbuch der physiologischen Optic.* Leipzig: L. Voss.

James, William. 1890. *The principles of psychology.* Vol. 1. Boston, MA: Henry Holt and Co.

Kress, G. and van Leeuwen, T. 1996. *Reading images: The grammar of visual design*. London: Routledge.

Kress, G. and Van Leeuwen, T. 2001. *Multimodal discourse: The modes and media of contemporary communication*. London: Edward Arnold.

Latour, B. 1994. On technical mediation. *Common Knowledge* 3(2), 29–64.

Latour, B. 1996. Do scientific objects have a history? Pasteur and Whitehead in a bath of lactic acid. *Common Knowledge* 5(1), 76–91.

Latour, B. 2005. *Reassembling the social: An introduction to actor-network-theory*. Oxford: Oxford University Press.

Levelt, W.J.M. 1989. *Speaking*. Cambridge, MA: MIT Press.

Norris, S. 2002. A theoretical framework for multimodal discourse analysis presented via the analysis of identity construction of two women living in Germany. Department of Linguistics: Georgetown University. Dissertation: UMI.

Norris, S. 2004a. *Analyzing multimodal interaction: A methodological framework*. London: Routledge.

Norris, S. 2004b. Multimodal discourse analysis: A conceptual framework. In: Levine, P. and Scollon, R. (eds.) *Discourse and technology: Multimodal discourse analysis*. Washington, DC: Georgetown University Press, 101–115.

Norris, S. 2005. Habitus, social identity, the perception of male domination – And agency? In: Norris, Sigrid and Jones, R. (eds.) *Discourse in action: Introducing mediated discourse analysis*. London: Routledge, 183–197.

Norris, S. 2006. Multiparty interaction: A multimodal perspective on relevance. *Discourse Studies* 8(3), 401–421.

Norris, S. 2008. Some thoughts on personal identity construction: A multimodal perspective. In: Bhatia, Vijay, Flowerdew, John, and Jones, Rodney H. (eds.) *New Directions* in Discourse. London: Routledge, 132–149.

Norris, S. 2011a. *Identity in (inter)action: Introducing multimodal (inter)action analysis*. Berlin and Boston, MA: deGruyter Mouton.

Norris, S. 2011b. Three hierarchical positions of deictic gesture in relation to spoken language: A multimodal interaction analysis. *Visual Communication* 10(2), 1–19.

Norris, S. 2013. What is a mode? Smell, olfactory perception, and the notion of mode in multimodal mediated theory. *Multimodal Communication* 2(2), 155–169.

Norris, S. (ed.) 2016. *Multimodality: Critical Concepts in Linguistics*. 1st ed. Volumes I–IV, 1,714 pages. Abingdon, UK: Routledge.

Norris, S. 2017. Scales of action: An example of driving & car talk in Germany and North America. *Text & Talk* 37(1), 117–139.

Norris, S. 2019. *Systematically working with multimodal data: Research methods in multimodal discourse analysis*. Hoboken, NJ: Wiley Blackwell.

Pashler, H.E. 1998. *The psychology of attention*. Cambridge, MA: MIT Press.

Sacks, H., Schegloff, E., and Jefferson, G. 1974. A simplest systematics for the organization of turn-taking for conversation. *Language* 50, 696–735.

Scollon, R. 1997. Handbills, tissues, and condoms: A site of engagement for the construction of identity in public discourse. *Journal of Sociolinguistics* 1(1), 39–61.

Scollon, R. 1998. *Mediated discourse as social interaction: A study of news discourse.* London: Longman.

Scollon, R. 2001a. *Mediated discourse: The nexus of practice.* London: Routledge.

Scollon, R. 2001b. Action and text: Toward an integrated understanding of the place of text in social (inter)action. In: Wodak, R. and Meyer, M. (eds.) *Methods of critical discourse analysis.* London: SAGE, 139–183.

Tannen, D. 1984. *Conversational style: Analyzing talk among friends.* Norwood, NJ: Ablex.

Tannen, D. and Wallat, C. 1993. Interactive frames and knowledge schemas in interaction: Examples from a medical examination/interview. In: Tannen, D. (ed.) *Framing in discourse.* New York and Oxford: Oxford University Press, 57–76.

Tse, P. 2005. Voluntary attention modulates the brightness of overlapping transparent surfaces. *Vision Research* 45(9), 1095–1098.

Van Leeuwen, T. 1999. *Speech, music, sound.* London: Macmillan Press.

Vygotsky, L.S. 1978. *Mind in society: The development of higher psychological processes*, eds. M. Cole, V. John-Steiner, S. Scribner, and E. Souberman. Cambridge, MA: Harvard University Press.

Wertsch, J.V. 1998. *Voices of the mind: A sociocultural approach to mediated action.* Cambridge, MA: Harvard University Press.

Wodak, R. 1989. *Language, power and ideology.* Amsterdam: Benjamins.

Wodak, R. 1995. Critical linguistics and critical discourse analysis. In: Verschueren, J., Östman, J.-O., and Blommaert, J. (eds.) *Handbook of pragmatics: Manual.* Amsterdam: Benjamins, 204–210.

Wodak, R. 2001. What CDA is about – A summary of its history, important concepts and its developments. In: Wodak, R. and Meyer, M. (eds.) *Methods of critical discourse analysis.* London: SAGE, 1–13.

Wu, W. 2011. What is conscious attention? *Philosophy and Phenomenological Research* 82, 93–120. doi:10.1111/j.1933-1592.2010.00457.x

Wu, W. 2014. *Attention.* London and New York: Routledge.

2 Examining Multimodal Action and Interaction
Theory and Analytical Tools

Introduction

Chapter 1 explicated the overarching notions of the framework, outlining multimodal (inter)action analysis, (inter)action, (inter)actional attention, mediation and mode. This chapter moves deeper into analytical tools for the analysis of actions and interactions. But upfront, a note that in multimodal discourse analysis we work in a systematic way as outlined in Norris (2019). This way of working is not replicated in this book. Rather, the chapters in this book focus in greater detail upon the theoretical and analytical concepts and tools explicated within. In many ways, it may be useful for the interested researcher to use the two books in tandem because the information is not replicated. In Norris (2019), some of the analytical tools that are discussed in this chapter are discussed from a different vantage point. There, I describe how to select analytical tools, how they are used and how they link to perception and embodiment.

This chapter is a detailed explication of theory and methodological tools. The chapter clearly details 12 concepts needed for the analysis of multimodal actions and interactions, listing for each in a gray textbox:

1 The history of the concept, that is, when and where it was developed and when and where it was first published. Based on this information, the reader can then go to the reference list and find detailed bibliographical information for further reading.
2 The theory that is embedded in the concept.
3 How the concept is used as an analytical tool to analyze data.
4 Brief practical example(s) elucidating the concept.
5 Some analytical capabilities of the concept.

The following text after each textbox of concise information goes into more detail about the concept, adding a longer example and/or a table and/or a graph to illustrate the concept further. Examples, some real and some envisioned, are used throughout merely to enhance comprehension of the analytical tools.

The chapter is brief, and the aim of the chapter is on the one hand to explicate the theoretical and analytical concepts used in multimodal (inter)action analysis; and on the other hand, to provide the reader with a guide for the analysis of everyday (inter)action. The data that can be analyzed using these tools may be video and audio recordings of social actors acting and interacting, or content from the Internet, movies, TV and so on. For possible data collection and a systematic way of working with the data, refer to Norris (2019) as such a discussion is outside the scope of this chapter.

Necessary Theoretical Background

The analytical tools discussed below build upon the following notions:

- All actions are mediated actions (Vygotsky 1978; Scollon 1998, 2001; Wertsch 1998). A mediated action is defined by Wertsch and Scollon as a social actor acting with or through mediational means/cultural tools. Discussions of mediated actions in relation to the analytical tools explicated in this book can be found in Norris and Jones (2005) and Norris (2004a, 2011, 2019).
- A mode is defined as a system of mediated action (Norris 2013).

Lower-level Mediated Action

History

Developed in Norris (2002a), first published in Norris (2004).

Theory

The lower-level mediated action is the smallest *interactional meaning unit* that a social actor uses and is able to read in interaction. Always mediated in multiple ways.

Analytical Tool

A single social actor produces a lower-level mediated action with or through multiple mediational means/cultural tools.

Examples

1   Peter says *"hi."*
2   Laura *points to the window* (moving the hand/arm from a rest position to a stroke and back to a rest position).
3   Mary *looks up from her computer screen at the student* standing in her office door (change of gaze).

Some Analytical Capabilities

1   Discovery of mediational means/cultural tools used in the production of a specific lower-level mediated action.
2   Discovery of how the lower-level mediated actions chain together in an interaction.
3   Necessary for transcription of multimodal (inter)action (see transcription conventions in Norris 2004a, 2011, 2019) as well as below.
4   Discovery of how lower-level mediated actions together produce specific modal density of a higher-level mediated action.
5   Discovery of how lower-level mediated actions and their chains produce specific modal configurations in an interaction.

The lower-level mediated action was developed in Norris (2002a) and first published in Norris (2004). The lower-level mediated action is defined as the smallest interactional (or pragmatic) meaning unit of a mode with a beginning and an end. Examples of a mode are language, gesture, gaze, posture, proxemics or walking. Chapter 1 already introduced the concepts of *mode* and *mediated action*, and the definitions are given also above. Just as all other mediated actions, the lower-level mediated action always consists of social actor acting with or through multiple mediational means/cultural tools. In early works (Norris 2002b, 2004a,b, 2005, 2006), the notion of mediation was briefly discussed and then often dropped in the writings as a given, since no action can be accomplished without being mediated. Thus, because of this viewpoint taken, the term "mediated" was often left out. Lately (Norris 2017a,b, 2019), however, the term "mediated" is being emphasized. The reason for this is the fact that we can learn much by analyzing in which ways a lower-level action is mediated since the mediational means/cultural tools used can give much insight into particular actions that social actors produce.

When watching a person walk (Figure 2.1), we can see that each step is a lower-level mediated action. A social actor can take just one step

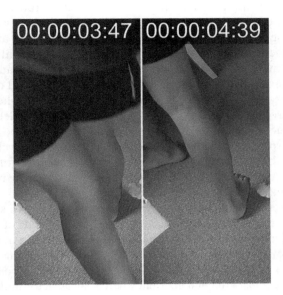

Figure 2.1 Walking: a chain of lower-level meditated action.

and thus produce one lower-level mediated action of the mode of walking. Or, a social actor can take many steps in a row. When we watch a social actor walking several steps, we can understand how lower-level mediated actions of the same kind build a chain. But even if a social actor takes only one step at one moment, a social actor will not stay in that same position forever and the mode of walking still builds a chain. Chaining of lower-level mediated actions is somewhat continuous in real life. In our research, the chains of lower-level mediated actions that we investigate depend upon our data and our focus of analysis (Norris 2019).

Figure 2.1 shows a woman taking a step. In the first image, we see her lifting her left leg as she is repositioning her weight onto her right foot. As soon as the left foot has been firmly planted on the ground, she begins to lift her right foot as can be seen in the second image. Here, she is already beginning to lift her right heel, thus beginning a new lower-level mediated action. In this way, lower-level mediated actions (here in form of walking) seamlessly appear to chain together. However, we can also delineate these chains into individual lower-level mediated actions, that is, one step at a time because this lower-level mediated action has a clear beginning and end point.

When analyzing the mediational means/cultural tools used in the production of a chain of lower-level mediated actions of walking, we find that the social actor (Figure 2.1) utilizes her legs, feet and the carpeted surface to take these steps. Furthermore, the social actor employs her knowledge about what it means to walk (instead of run or dance, for example), how it feels to walk on carpet (instead of on pavement or in sand, for example) and how the foot is placed when walking barefoot around an object (instead of in heels, for example). Thus, we find a range of mediational means/cultural tools from bodily physical to environmentally physical and from cognitive to psychological.[1] Neither of these is more important than another. Rather, for the social actor shown in Figure 2.1 to walk in the way she does, she needs to be able to utilize all of these simultaneously.

Just as steps build chains of lower-level mediated actions, so do utterances, gaze shifts, postural shifts and so on. These chains of lower-level mediated actions can be traced in moments that we find in our data. But chains of lower-level mediated actions may also begin at one point and be taken up by the same social actors at a very different point in time. For example, I just attended an event where a social actor took up a conversation from 20 years ago. Nobody without a connection to the actual conversation was able to make any sense of what the social actor was referring to. Whereas those who had been engaged in the actual conversation 20 years ago took it up as if the conversation had just occurred a few days earlier. The lower-level mediated actions of the mode of language, the utterances, thus had chained across a long timescale (Lemke 2000a,b). Some conversations can continue over a lifetime and even over many lifetimes, while other conversations (such as transactions) may be brief and may be completed in short timescales so that the beginnings and endings of these chains can be clearly delineated. Noteworthy is that the length of a pause between one lower-level mediated action and another lower-level mediated action can vary widely within a chain of lower-level mediated actions as well as across various chains of lower-level mediated actions.

While the notion of timescales needs to be remembered, for us as researchers the lower-level mediated action is of utmost importance because it allows us, for example, to

1   Delineate one lower-level mediated action at a time (bracketed by pauses)
2   Analyze which mediational means/cultural tools are utilized in the lower-level mediated action under study
3   Analyze how certain kinds of lower-level mediated actions chain together in interaction.

Table 2.1 shows how the notion of the lower-level mediated action allows us to analyze very different kinds of actions in a theoretically congruent manner. In other words, because of the unit of analysis, the lower-level mediated action, we can analyze all modes that are utilized by social actors in (inter)action in a theoretically founded manner even though all modes have very different structures and consist of different materiality (see also Norris 2004a).

Here, when we analyze the lower-level mediated action of the mode of spoken language, we can look at it from two different sides: either we can investigate how and when an utterance is bracketed by in-breath, or depending upon our data, we may want to examine how and when the in-breath is bracketed by an utterance (or a sound made by the person). The first way of examining will focus us upon the language, while the second way focuses us upon the production of silence. Similarly, arm/hand/finger movements are bracketed by stillness of the arm/hand/fingers, and stillness of the arm/hand/fingers is bracketed by movements of the arm/hand/fingers.

Table 2.1 Some modes and their lower-level mediated actions

Mode	Lower-level mediated actions	
Spoken language	**Utterance** Bracketed by in-breath	**Breath** Bracketed by utterances
Gesture	**All arm/hand/finger movements** Bracketed by stillness	**Stillness of arm/hand/fingers** Bracketed by arm/hand/finger movements
Gaze	**Gaze shifts** Moving the eyes from point A to point B Bracketed by gazing at one point	**Gazing at a point** Bracketed by gaze shifts
Posture	**Postural shifts** Moving the body from point A to point B Bracketed by stillness	**Postural stillness** Bracketed by postural shifts
Walking	**Step** Lifting one foot and moving it from point A to point B at a walking pace Bracketed by lifting the other foot or by standing	**Standing** Bracketed movements
Smell	**Sniff** A particular in-breath to determine the smell of something Bracketed by no particular sniffs	**Continued smelling** Bracketed by sniffs

Figure 2.2 Lower-level mediated actions bracketed either by movement or by stillness.

What we see here is that each lower-level mediated action is bracketed by another connected lower-level mediated action (Figure 2.2).

When looking at Table 2.1, we can continue the table as we need in order to illuminate our data. For example, we may be examining a data piece of a runner as they are training. Here, we may wish to examine the chains of lower-level mediated actions to see how the social actor is switching between running and walking. By transcribing the transition between running and walking, we can then determine exactly how the transition occurs and see exactly when and how the runner has changed the pace to a walking or a running stride. Here, we would view the running stride being bracketed by the walking stride and the walking stride as being bracketed by the running stride.

Lower-level Mediated Actions and Modes

Modes are the abstracted level of concretely performed lower-level mediated actions (see Chapter 1 for the definition and description of mode). Let us take language as our first example: A social actor visiting a foreign country for a long time listens to the surrounding social actors, and after a while begins to speak their first words in this new language. These words are reacted to by others and, in turn, the social actor learns to speak more words and sentences. As we know, social actors learn language in and through social interaction. The longer the social actor resides in the foreign country, interacting with native speakers, the more their new mode of language (or the system of mediated action new to the social actor) develops. But the social actor does not only learn language. They also learn how to hold and utilize their posture; how to gaze at points in the environment, objects and faces; or how to walk in the foreign country. Each of these modes is learned in and through the actions and interactions that the social actor engages in. When we now briefly revisit the notion of (inter)action discussed in the previous chapter, we realize that modes are learned with and through (inter)action with other social actors, with the environment and with objects. Thus, each mode is acquired in and through (inter)action. Figure 2.3 illustrates the levels from concrete

	Concepts	Examples
Abstracted	Mode of spoken language = A system of mediated action	Beatrice speaking
Concrete	Lower-level mediated action = Producing one utterance	(1) Beatrice: I love this coffee

Figure 2.3 Concrete (action) and abstracted (mode) levels.

to abstracted, where the concrete level builds the foundation and the abstracted level sits above.

However, modes (or systems of mediated actions) are never acquired alone. Rather one mode is acquired together with other modes. For example, the mode of spoken language is acquired in tandem with the modes of gaze, object handling and/or proxemics. Or, the mode of spoken language may be acquired in tandem with posture, gesture and/or music. In fact, it is acquired with many different constellations of modes, depending upon the situation, the social actors present (or absent), and the environment and objects within.

The interesting thing about the term *mode*, when theorized as systems of mediated action, is that it allows us to see how modal learning in one situation is transferrable to another very different situation. An utterance or word learned when playing cards is later transferred to ordering at a restaurant, for example. This kind of transferability is unlike transferability of practices. While a practice [such as handing as discussed in detail by Scollon (2001)] is an abstracted mediated action with a history and the practice can be utilized at different sites of engagement, the practice does not quickly change drastically. Rather, a practice is a practice specifically because it exhibits a great deal of similarity. Whereas the utilization of a mode such as language, gaze or touch can be drastically different when playing cards than when sitting in a restaurant. Thus, here the context allows for, and even dictates, drastically different uses of the modes, drastically different constellations of the modes that are produced together and drastically different meanings that therefore are being produced.

Multimodal Transcription Conventions

History

First developments of multimodal transcription in Norris (2002b). Then development of multimodal transcription conventions in Norris (2002a). Transcription conventions first published in Norris (2004a).

Theory

Transcription conventions are based on the lower-level mediated action, the smallest *interactional meaning unit* that a social actor uses and is able to read in interaction. Each lower-level mediated action has a clear beginning and end.

Analytical Tool

A single social actor's production of a lower-level mediated action is transcribed by illustrating the beginning and the ending points of the lower-level mediated action with a time-stamped still image. Sometimes, midpoints are also shown.

First, modal transcripts are produced. Then modal transcripts are collated to produce a final multimodal transcript (based on the time-stamps).

By transcribing interaction in this way, we find that modal production in interaction does not adhere to clock-time. Clock-time only comes into play for the researcher when producing and collating transcripts.

Examples

See Norris (2004a, 2011, 2019) for detailed transcription examples.

Some Analytical Capabilities

1   Discovery of how multiple chains of lower-level mediated action are produced by social actors through different rhythms simultaneously.
2   Discovery of how some chains of lower-level mediated actions synchronize in (inter)action.
3   Discovery of how some lower-level mediated actions are bracketed by longer pauses in (inter)action.
4   Discovery of how some lower-level mediated actions are produced in quick succession in (inter)action.
5   Discovery of how several chains of lower-level mediated actions co-occur in (inter)action without being synchronized.
6   Discoveries in liaison with the myriad of analytical tools outlined in this book.

Multimodal transcription conventions based on the lower-level mediated actions were first developed in Norris (2002a) and first published in Norris (2004a). Since the lower-level mediated action is defined as the smallest (inter)actional (or pragmatic) meaning unit with a beginning and an ending point, the lower-level mediated action is the perfect unit for the production of transcription. As mentioned above, examples of a mode[2] are language, gesture, gaze, posture, proxemics or walking. When having a look at the lower-level mediated actions in Figure 2.2, we find that each arm/hand/finger movement is bracketed by stillness of the arm/hand/fingers. Just as we find that arm/hand/finger stillness is bracketed by arm/hand/finger movements.

In multimodal transcripts, we focus our view on the movements that a social actor produces. By transcribing the movements in an interaction, we, at the very same time, embed the stillness of the social actor in the multimodal transcript. Due to the timestamp on the top left corner of each still, both the length of movement and the length of stillness are clearly illustrated in the transcripts.

Clock-time is thus built into the transcripts (through time-stamps) without, however, driving transcription. Rather, clock-time is first used to produce collated transcripts, and second, clock-time is used to examine how long or short certain lower-level mediated actions proceed in relation to others. By transcribing the movements and thereby the pauses that a social actor produces, we transcribe the (inter)action as closely as possible to the actual unfolding of the (inter)action, distilling what can be distilled in order to make better sense of the complexity involved. Important to remember is that by transcribing one movement at a time, we also transcribe stillness.

As Table 2.2 shows, the notion of the lower-level mediated action allows us to transcribe very different kinds of actions in a theoretically congruent manner. In other words, because of the unit of analysis, the lower-level mediated action, we can transcribe all modes that are utilized by social actors in an interaction in a theoretically founded manner even though all modes have very different structures and consist of different materiality. Our transcripts are very focused as outlined in detail in the way of systematically working with multimodal data, i.e., it is important to note here that *we do not begin our analysis with transcription* (see Norris, 2019, for details of when transcripts are produced in the analysis process).

Certainly, one may transcribe more than the lower-level mediated actions indicated in Table 2.2. One may be examining an (inter)action, in which a social actor frequently moves their feet. In that case, a leg/foot movement transcript (see Norris 2019) will need to be produced. Or there may be other movements that need to be transcribed in order

Table 2.2 Some multimodal transcription conventions

Multimodal transcription conventions
Utterance   Transcribe the utterances
Arm/hand/finger movements   Take a snapshot of the beginning and the endpoint of the movement (sometimes an image of the midpoint is also useful)
Gaze shifts   Take a snapshot of the beginning and the endpoint of the gaze shift
Postural shifts   Take a snapshot of the beginning and the endpoint of the postural shift
Step   Take a snapshot of the beginning and the endpoint of the step
Sniff   Take a snapshot of the beginning and the endpoint of the sniff
Movements of the head   Take a snapshot of the beginning and the endpoint of the head movement
Shoulder movement   Take a snapshot of the beginning and the endpoint of the shoulder movement
Facial expression   Take a snapshot of the beginning and the endpoint of the change in facial expression (sometimes an image at a midpoint is useful here)
Proxemic shift   Take a snapshot of the beginning and the endpoint of the proxemic shift
Producing a collated multimodal transcript   Use the time-stamps on the images to collate modal transcripts. First, you collate two modal transcripts (such as gaze and head movement), then add another (such as gesture), etc.   Use arrows, numbers, circles, etc. to show details without having to show too many stills in one collated transcript.

to best represent the (inter)action that one is studying. The lower-level mediated action is the unit of analysis that allows the production of transcripts that go beyond what is discussed here because it allows the researcher to work in a theoretically congruent manner with any kind of multimodal data displaying actions and interactions.

Important to realize is that the lower-level mediated action, which is our basis for multimodal transcription, is an analytical unit. While we *can analyze* individual lower-level mediated actions, we want to realize that *no social actor ever performs just one lower-level mediated action.*

For example, we can transcribe and analyze a specific gesture that a participant in a study performs, but while the participant performs the gesture, they also hold their body in a certain way, look at something, hold or move their feet and so on. Lower-level mediated actions *always* come together in action and interaction, producing (and being produced by) higher-level mediated actions. As analysts, we can certainly tease the various chains and their individual lower-level mediated actions apart and analyze exactly how they are being produced. But when social actors act and interact, they *always produce higher-level mediated actions*, which come together and produce the various lower-level mediated actions and the chains that they form.

Higher-level Mediated Action

History

Developed in Norris (2002a), first published in Norris (2004a).

Theory

The coming together of multiple chains of lower-level mediated action builds a higher-level mediated action. Simultaneously, the higher-level mediated action that a social actor produces builds the multiple chains of lower-level mediated action. Higher- and lower-level mediated actions thus produce each other through actions and interactions.

Analytical Tool

A single social actor produces a higher-level mediated action through the coming together of multiple chains of lower-level mediated actions. No two people produce a co-constructed higher-level mediated action through the exact same chaining of lower-level mediated actions.

Examples

Peter and Mary are having dinner.
    Gary is mowing the lawn.
    A person, even if not or only partially visible, is explaining something in a YouTube clip.

Some Analytical Capabilities

1. Discovery of which chains of lower-level mediated actions are used by each participant in the production of a specific higher-level mediated action.
2. Discovery of how the higher-level mediated actions produced by each social actor involved come together in co-produced (inter)actions.
3. Discovery of how social actors pay more or less attention to several higher-level mediated actions at a time.
4. Discovery of how focused upon, mid- and backgrounded higher-level mediated actions are shared or not shared in co-produced (inter)action.
5. Discovery of the modal density of specific higher-level mediated actions for each social actor involved in a co-produced (inter)action.
6. Discovery of the modal configurations produced by each social actor in a co-produced (inter)action.
7. Discovery that each social actor on their own can and does produce higher-level mediated actions when (inter)acting with the environment or objects.

The higher-level mediated action was developed in Norris (2002a) and first published in Norris (2004a). The higher-level mediated action is defined as the coming together of multiple chains of lower-level mediated actions. As soon as we begin to analyze through which chains of lower-level mediated actions a higher-level mediated action is produced by social actors, we can also examine how each chain of lower-level mediated action that partially builds the higher-level mediated action is mediated in multiple ways.

Further, when realizing that social actors produce a multitude of chains of lower-level mediated actions when producing a higher-level mediated action, we can learn to understand how various social actors co-produce the ostensibly same higher-level mediated action in vastly different ways. Certainly, multimodal intersubjectivity (Pirini 2016) is achieved in co-produced higher-level mediated actions. Yet, the actual higher-level mediated actions that each social actor produces in the (inter)action differs. Once we analyze each social actor's higher-level mediated actions, we can then analyze how the various simultaneously produced higher-level mediated actions by each social actor differ in modal density, allowing us to investigate social actors' phenomenologically displayed attention states as explained below.

When engaging in a Skype conversation (a higher-level mediated action), we can see that each social actor produces a different higher-level mediated action through different chains of lower-level mediated actions. Thus, a co-produced higher-level mediated action of Skyping differs in the production of chains of lower-level mediated actions that each social actor produces. Just as chains of lower-level mediated actions that belong to one higher-level mediated action can be produced with and/or through large pauses, so can higher-level mediated actions develop across long timescales (Lemke 2000a,b).

As researchers the higher-level mediated action is of utmost importance because it allows us for example to:

1   Delineate one higher-level mediated action at a time (bracketed by beginnings and endings determined by the researcher).
2   Analyze which chains of lower-level mediated actions are utilized in and for the higher-level mediated action under scrutiny.
3   Analyze how different social actors produce the ostensibly same higher-level mediated action differently.

As Table 2.3 shows, the notion of the higher-level mediated action allows us to analyze very different kinds of actions in a theoretically congruent manner. In other words, because of the unit of analysis, the higher-level mediated action and the chains of lower-level mediated actions that produce the higher-level mediated action at the same time as they are produced by the higher-level mediated action, we can analyze the complexity of interactions in a theoretically founded manner.

Higher-level Mediated Actions and Practices

Higher-level mediated actions also build practices, which are defined by Scollon (1998) as actions with a history. Figure 2.4 illustrates the concrete and abstracted levels, with the concrete level building the foundation.

Here, we see how the abstracted level of practice emerges directly from concrete higher-level mediated actions that social actors perform and, at the very same time, how the abstracted level of practice enforces how certain actions are performed by social actors. In other words, a person new to having coffee learns to have coffee with a specific social actor in a specific way. By doing so, the person also learns to have coffee with different people in different circumstances. But we also need to consider that others enforce what it means to have coffee. If the person instead of having coffee or some other drink begins to eat

Table 2.3 Some higher-level mediated actions and some possible chains of lower-level mediated actions to make up and produce the higher-level mediated action

Higher-level mediated action	*Chains of lower-level mediated action*
Conversation	**Chains of** Utterances—breaths Arm/hand/finger movements—stillness of arms/hands/fingers Gaze shifts—gazing at a point—closing eyes Postural shifts—postural stillness Proxemic shifts—proxemic stillness Leg/foot movements—leg/foot stillness
Skype conversation	**Chains of** Utterances Hand–arm movements Mouse movements Technology adjustments Gaze shifts Postural shifts
Having dinner	**Chains of** Object handling (serving/taking food, using utensils) Chewing Utterances Gaze shifts Postural shifts Sniffs Tasting Facial expression

	Concepts	**Examples**
Abstracted	Practice = An action with a history	Anybody having a cup coffee with anybody else
Concrete	Higher-level mediated action = One-time concrete action	Beatrice having a cup of coffee with Tim

Figure 2.4 Concrete higher-level mediated action and its abstracted practice level.

lunch, others will not consider this action as having coffee. Here, others, who have internalized the practice of having coffee will reinforce the practice by at least commenting on the difference between having coffee and lunch. But when the person new to having coffee indeed has coffee with another, the concrete higher-level mediated action of having coffee at that particular time with that particular other social actor in that particular place adheres to and reinforces the abstracted practice level. This notion will be taken up again below, under the heading of site of engagement.

Lower Scale Higher-Level Mediated Actions and Practices

Higher-level mediated actions can be found at various scales from a very low (or small) scale such as *handing* to a larger scale of *having coffee* described above, or a much larger scale such as having a career over many years. Here, I would like to particularly point out the lower scale higher-level mediated action and the (lower scale) practices in order to distinguish them from the lower-level mediated action and the abstracted level of *mode*.

A lower scale higher-level mediated action, just as any other higher-level mediated action, builds and is reinforced by practices. A lower scale higher-level mediated action, again just like any other higher-level mediated action, comes about and produces several chains of lower-level mediated actions that are coming together. An example is given in Figure 2.5, where we find the lower scale higher-level mediated action of handing on the foundational concrete level and the (lower scale) practice on the abstracted level on top.

Lower scale higher-level mediated actions thus also build practices, which are defined by Scollon (1998) as actions with a history. Here, we see how the abstracted level of practice emerges directly through lower scale higher-level mediated actions that social actors perform; and, at the very same time, how the abstracted level of practice enforces how certain actions are performed by social actors. In other words, a child learns to hand a specific object to a caregiver. By doing so, the child

	Concepts	**Examples**
Abstracted	(Lower scale) Practice = An action with a history	Anybody handing anything to anybody else
Concrete	(Lower scale) Higher-level mediated action = One-time concrete action	Person A handing a cup to person B

Figure 2.5 Concrete lower scale higher-level mediated action and its abstracted practice level.

learns to hand different objects to different people [for a detailed account, see Scollon (2001)]. But we also need to consider that a caregiver enforces what it means that a child hands an object. If the child throws the object, that is not considered *handing*, and the caregiver will demonstrate how the object needs to change from one person's hand to another's in order to count as handing. Here, the caregiver, who has internalized the practice of handing is enforcing the practice upon the child, who, in turn is learning *how to hand correctly*. Important to note is that neither the concrete action of handing an object to another, nor the practice of handing are separate in an instance of handing. Rather, they always come together at a site of engagement (Scollon 1998) as we will see below.

As mentioned earlier, modes differ from practices in that modal knowledge allows for drastically different modal use for different social actors in different sites of engagement. Whereas practices exhibit the notion of sameness and social correctness to a relatively narrow extent, modal use has a much wider spectrum of difference without losing social correctness. When thinking about a little boy, who has learned the practice of handing, and who is handing a perfume bottle to a caregiver, we can see that all handing has a great extent of sameness to it in order to allow for social correctness. However, it does not matter whether the little boy feels the intricately cut-glass perfume bottle while handing it to the caregiver (see Norris, 2013, for a more detailed description of such actions). How he experiences the mode of touch has no impact upon the practice of handing. In fact, the mode of touch and his experience of it can vary widely depending upon different objects; just as the mode of touch may differ greatly between various social actors without having much or even any impact upon social correctness and the performance of the higher-level mediated action of handing, which is enforced and/or changed through and with the concrete instantiation of the action.[3]

Frozen Mediated Actions

History

Developed in Norris (2002a), first published in Norris (2004a).

Theory

As humans we understand the world around us as acted upon by social actors. Therefore, lower-level mediated actions and higher-level mediated actions are embedded in the environment and in objects.

Analytical Tool

A single lower-level mediated action (such as a brush stroke in a painting) and higher-level mediated action (such as a picture having been placed in a specific spot) are entailed in a painting itself.

Examples

A *brush stroke* is frozen (embedded) in the painting itself.
A painting *hung up in a specific spot* is frozen in where it is placed.

Some Analytical Capabilities

1   Discovery of how social actors read mediated actions off of objects and/or the environment.
2   Discovery of which lower-level or higher-level mediated actions are entailed foremost and which are entailed in a more hidden way.
3   Important in the transcription of multimodal interaction [see transcription conventions in Norris (2004a, 2011 or 2019) and above].

The frozen mediated action was developed in Norris (2002a) and first published in Norris (2004a). The frozen mediated action is defined as the lower- or higher-level mediated action embedded in the environment or in objects. When thinking of the environment and objects in terms of mediated actions, we begin to analyze how social actors in their everyday lives understand their surroundings. The environment, think of a building for example, was produced in the way that it is now through social actors' mediated actions, or, think of some wild forest, which was left as it is now because of social actors' mediated actions taken or not taken. Or think of the way you are dressed at this moment. Whatever you are wearing entails the very mediated actions that you had to perform to dress in this way. Now, the way you are dressed is a frozen higher-level mediated action and this frozen action is linked to some practice as are all other higher-level mediated actions as discussed above.

As soon as we begin to analyze the environment and objects as entailing frozen mediated actions either of a lower level (think about art historians inspecting an old painting and examining the individual brush strokes) or of a higher level (think of a painting that has been found in a dark cave), we realize that in our human way of thinking, all mediated actions are produced by social actors.

Further, when realizing that the environment and objects embed mediated actions that some social actors have produced at an earlier time, we can learn to understand how time and rhythms play a role in frozen mediated actions. For example, when we walk into an empty classroom, we can tell much about the (inter)actions that went on before we entered the space now empty of social actors. Seating arrangements, forgotten pieces of paper, unwiped whiteboards, all tell of the actions and interactions even when we do not actually know the social actors who had participated in the classroom (inter)action previously. Mediated actions are frozen in the environment and frozen in the objects within. Figures 2.6 and 2.7 illustrate how the frozen lower- and higher-level mediated actions link to the abstracted levels of mode and practice.

When looking at Figures 2.6 and 2.7, the question of how the concept of mode differs from the concept of practice becomes evident.

	Concepts	Examples
Abstracted	Mode of painting	Brushstrokes in paintings
Concrete	Frozen lower-level mediated action	An artist's brushstroke visible in a painting

Figure 2.6 Concrete frozen lower-level mediated action and abstracted mode level.

	Concepts	Examples
Abstracted	Practice	Paintings hung up on walls in homes
Concrete	Frozen higher-level mediated action	A painting hung on a wall in a home

Figure 2.7 Concrete frozen higher-level mediated action and its abstracted practice level.

Difference between Modes and Practices

Modes, defined as systems of mediated action, are knowledge accumulations of lower-level mediated actions. Whereas practices are higher-level mediated actions with a history.

As mentioned earlier, no one can ever perform just one lower-level mediated action alone: A social actor, due to the body, always performs numerous lower-level mediated actions simultaneously. For example, you hold your head in a certain way (lower-level mediated action of head movement), look at something (lower-level mediated action of gaze), hold your body in a certain way (lower-level mediated action of posture), point to a particular place ahead of you (lower-level mediated action of gesture) and speak (lower-level mediated action of spoken language) and so on. The concrete actions that you thus perform are simultaneous and always produce (or are produced by) a higher-level mediated action.

The production of higher-level mediated actions are, in part, enforced by practices, and at the very same time the production of a higher-level mediated action can change or reinforce the practice. In this way, concrete higher-level mediated actions reside on the micro (or concrete) level, while the practices reside on the meso (or abstracted) level. Practices exhibit notions of similarity and normativity, so that when a concrete higher-level mediated action is performed in alignment with a particular practice, the two levels merge.

While practices are abstractions of higher-level mediated actions, modes are abstractions of concrete lower-level mediated actions, which can never be performed alone, that is, are always a part of a higher-level mediated action. In order to grasp the notion of mode, we can think of language. When learning a new language, for example, we may memorize a word at the same time as we are trying to produce a sentence. Learning an individual word is a lower-level mediated action. This newly learned word can then later be used in a great variety of ways, moving past the sentence that we constructed while learning this word. At later times, this word, which was acquired through learning it, is not limited to a particular practice. Rather, it may be useful to a great number of practices, always, however, used in connection with different words, producing very different higher-level mediated actions. The word becomes a part of our abstract system of mediated actions, the mode of language. The more words we learn, the more developed our mode of language will be. The same is true for all other modes. We can learn dance steps (developing the mode of dance), ways to hold our body (developing the mode of posture) or brushstrokes (developing the mode of painting). Each time we learn to perform one lower-level mediated action, this lower-level mediated action is transferrable from one higher-level mediated action to others (see also Norris 2013).

Whereas when we learn a higher-level mediated action of dressing for a formal occasion for example, we learn a practice. But this higher-level mediated action can only be used in ways so that it links appropriately to formal occasions (or not, when making fun of the very practice). In a way, a practice (a higher-level mediated action with a history), which is socio-culturally and historically embedded, exists prior to an individual learning it. Thus, a practice is more static in the sense that there is a right and a wrong way of performing a particular higher-level mediated action linked to that practice. This differs greatly from the acquisition of a mode. While a mode is also socio-culturally and historically embedded, a mode is more linked to the individual and there is, for example, no right or wrong way of feeling a dog's fur (the mode of touch/feel), while there are right and wrong ways of petting a dog (the practice). There is no right or wrong way of producing a brushstroke on a canvas (the mode of painting), but when producing art (the practice) certain ways of how brushstrokes are positioned on a painting play a role. While art practice is always searching out the new, there are nevertheless certain agreed upon ways of doing art, and, of course, doing art does not only depend upon the placement of brushstrokes (a chain of lower-level mediated action of the mode of painting), but many other chains of lower-level mediated action of other modes that come together to *correctly* perform a higher-level mediated action that links to the art practice. This is similar to learning a language. While you can certainly learn many different words (concrete lower-level mediated actions) and increase your knowledge of the *mode* of language, there are certain situations when you can or cannot use a particular word (as a part of a concrete higher-level mediated action) to communicate in a social practice *appropriate* way. Putting it differently, your learning words of a foreign language enhances your knowledge of the mode of language. Whereas your use of words in a social situation illustrates your knowledge of a given practice.

A practice is the abstracted level of a concrete higher-level mediated action, which is always produced through the coming together of a multitude of concrete chained lower-level mediated actions. By performing a concrete higher-level mediated action that links to (often by others) previously performed higher-level mediated actions, the concrete action is linked to a practice, whereas a mode is the abstracted level of a concrete lower-level mediated action. By performing a concrete lower-level mediated action, a social actor accumulates knowledge about the mode itself, thus building up their own system of mediated actions (or modes).

Modal Aggregate

History

First published in Norris (2009a).

Theory

Modal aggregates are the tightly coming together (of often chains) of lower-level mediated actions within higher-level mediated actions. This means that several modes have to closely come together for the higher-level mediated action to unfold as it does.

Analytical Tool

We analyze how a social actor produces *certain* modal aggregates in an interaction when producing higher-level mediated actions.

Examples

When Ken is speaking on his mobile with high modal density, mobile phone use is just as important a mode as is the mode of spoken language (his utterances) since without his use of the phone, the conversation would not unfold as it does. But this aggregate constellation is not the case for everyone making a phone call. Some people will not produce an aggregate here. Aggregates are not essential and are not something that we can assume. Every higher-level mediated action has to be analyzed to see how and if aggregates are being produced (see Norris 2014).

When Zoe is knitting a sweater with an intricate pattern, the modes of knitting, written language and the images that direct her in how to knit the intricate pattern build a modal aggregate since neither knitting alone, nor reading the pattern alone would allow her to produce the actions that she produces. But again, this is only an example, and this will not be the same for everybody knitting a sweater with an intricate pattern.

Some Analytical Capabilities

1 Discovery of how particular chains of lower-level mediated actions have to be intricately linked to produce a particular higher-level mediated action.
2 Discovery of how modal aggregates can tell of a social actor's knowledge of the performance of a particular higher-level mediated action.

Modal aggregate is a concept that relates to higher-level mediated actions. Modal aggregate is a concept that allows us to analyze which chains of lower-level mediated actions have to come tightly interlinked together in order for an action to take place in the way that it does. As mentioned above, we readily can tell if a social actor is focused upon a phone call, because they utilize the mode of spoken language with great intensity (producing chains of lower-level mediated actions, the utterances, with great intensity). But, when we now use the notion of modal aggregates, we quickly realize that the most important mode here is not spoken language, but rather it is the modal aggregate built through the mode spoken language in connection with the mode of mobile phone use. Thus here, together these modes build what we call a modal aggregate since the action of making a phone call can neither be accomplished without the device or the language. Similarly, if the social actor messaged the person, instead, using the very same phone, we can determine that object handling and typing as well as mobile phone use play an equal role in the mediated action. However, which modal aggregates are produced has to be determined through analysis. Sometimes, the production of modal aggregates can tell of a deep understanding of what the action is that is being produced (let us take Ken making a phone call on his mobile), while at other times, producing an aggregate can demonstrate that the social actor is not very advanced in producing the higher-level mediated action (let us take Zoe, knitting the sweater with an intricate pattern).

Modal Density

History

Developed in Norris (2002a), first published in Norris (2004a).

Theory

The coming together of chained lower-level mediated actions builds various types of density when a social actor performs a particular higher-level mediated action. Modal density is a short form for lower-level mediated action density.

Analytical Tool

When a social actor performs a higher-level mediated action, modal density can be analyzed as either being of intensity or of complexity through interconnectedness of chains of lower-level mediated actions or both. Modal density of a particular higher-level mediated action becomes apparent once the analyst has successfully delineated the higher-level action from others being performed and becomes clearly identifiable during multimodal transcription.[4]

Examples

Ken is speaking about an important topic on his mobile.
Zoe is knitting a sweater with a very intricate and difficult pattern.

Some Analytical Capabilities

1 Discovery of the weight of various modes (or better chains of lower-level mediated action) in the performance of a particular higher-level mediated action.
2 Discovery of how the lower-level mediated actions chain together as they are producing/being produced by the particular higher-level mediated action, displaying a certain modal density.
3 Discovery of the ways in which some chains of lower-level mediated actions actually build an intricate and sometimes even a most important part in the higher-level mediated action.
4 Discovery of the fact that social actors often produce several simultaneous higher-level mediated actions with different amounts of modal density. This leads to a discovery of attention/awareness levels in interaction (see "Modal Density Foreground–Background Continuum of Attention/ Awareness" below).

We all know when another person is focused upon some action or interaction. We also all know when someone pays less or even very little attention to an action or interaction. However, before the concept of modal density was developed, we could not explain why or how we know.

Modal density is the lower-level mediated action density with which a social actor produces a particular higher-level mediated action. When a social actor produces a particular chain of lower-level mediated actions with great intensity (such as the utterances in a phone call), then this intensity demonstrates to all around that this social actor is focused upon the phone call (high modal density). Similarly, if a social actor is focused upon decorating an elaborate cake, the social actor demonstrates this focus through the interconnectedness between a number of chains of lower-level mediated actions (such as moving the hand to add decorations, gazing at the cake, turning the cake with the other hand, etc.). Here, again, the focus of the social actor decorating the cake is apparent to the onlooker because of the modal density that the social actor produces. Other examples of social actors paying less attention to an action or interaction are given below in the "Modal Density Foreground–Background Continuum of Attention/Awareness" section.

The important thing to remember is that the modal density of a higher-level mediated action is readable and analyzable. As mentioned above, all actions and interactions that are performed are by nature higher-level mediated actions, which always are produced through a multitude of (often chains of) lower-level mediated actions.

Modal Configuration

History

First published in Norris (2009a).

Theory

Modal configuration is the hierarchical ordering of lower-level mediated actions in higher-level mediated actions. This means that some modes are of more and some modes are of less importance for the higher-level mediated action to unfold as it does.

Analytical Tool

A social actor produces certain modal configurations in interaction when producing higher-level mediated actions. Modal configurations can change quickly, making it often important to examine small scale higher-level mediated actions.

Examples

When Ken is speaking on his mobile with high modal density, the modal aggregate of mobile use and spoken language takes on the hierarchical position since without either, the conversation would not unfold *as it does.*

When Zoe is knitting the sweater, the modal aggregate of *object handling—written language—images* takes up the hierarchically superior position, while her posture, for example sits in a subordinate position.

Some Analytical Capabilities

1   Discovery of hierarchies of lower-level mediated actions and their chains in (inter)action.
2   Discovery of modal aggregates (i.e., modes that necessarily have to be produced together and that are intertwined to the extent that the mediated action cannot be produced in this way without them building an aggregate, see above).
3   Discovery of how specific modal configurations display the knowledge of a social actor.
4   Discovery of where the mode of language (or any other mode) actually sits in hierarchical terms within a specific higher-level mediated action in relation to other modes.

The concept of modal configurations relates to higher-level mediated actions and modal density, that is, modal intensity and modal complexity as well as modal aggregates. First of all, this concept relates to higher-level mediated actions, because no social actor can just produce one lower-level mediated action. Social actors always and only produce higher-level mediated actions. Second, the concept relates to modal density in that we delve deeper into the analysis of how modal density, that is, either intensity or complexity or a combination of the two, is achieved in action and interaction. Third, it relates to the concept of modal aggregate in that quite often in actions and interactions several chains of lower-level mediated actions (including frozen lower-level mediated actions) have to come together for a certain action to be produced in the way it is.

By hierarchizing modes (or chains of lower-level mediated actions), we can then determine where and how a mode such as language plays into an action or interaction. This can lead to new discoveries about modes such as language, touch, object handling and so on.

Modal Density Foreground–Background Continuum of Attention/Awareness

History

Developed in Norris (2002a), first published in Norris (2004a).

Theory

Social actors often produce more than one higher-level mediated action, even though only one focused higher-level mediated action can be produced at a time. A higher-level mediated action produced by a social actor through high modal density, in relation to other higher-level mediated actions performed simultaneously, displays their focus. The less attention a social actor pays to a certain higher-level mediated action, the lower the modal density.

Simultaneously performed higher-level mediated actions can be placed on a heuristic foreground–background continuum of attention/awareness.

Analytical Tool

When a social actor performs several higher-level mediated actions at the same time, the modal density of each one can be analyzed. First, the analyst realizes the various higher-level mediated actions as distinct from one another. Then, the analyst discovers the modal intensity or complexity or both during multimodal transcription. Once modal density of all higher-level mediated actions is discovered, the analyst utilizes the heuristic and places the simultaneously performed higher-level mediated actions relationally on the foreground–background continuum of attention/awareness.

Examples

Laurence is reading the newspaper and is talking to his partner about her day.

Karen is driving to the supermarket to buy groceries and talks with her children about their homework.

Some Analytical Capabilities

1   Discovery of social actors producing several higher-level mediated actions at a time.
2   Discovery of how social actors produce various modal densities in the performance of various simultaneously produced higher-level mediated actions, illustrating the attention/awareness levels.
3   Discovery that social actors in a co-produced higher-level mediated action may not produce the action at the same level of attention/awareness.
4   Discovery of the fact that social actors when paying different levels of attention to the same higher-level mediated

action may communicate well without both focusing on the same higher-level mediated action.

5   Discovery of the fact that social actors when paying the same amount of attention to the same higher-level mediated action may have trouble communicating.

6   Discovery of the fact that mutual focus in interaction is not necessarily preferred.

When social actors go about their everyday lives, all actions seem to be meshed together and co-produced with all others around. However, when taking the modal density foreground–background continuum as our analytical tool, we find that social actors co-produce higher-level mediated actions without necessarily all focusing upon the same action. Each individual involved in the same higher-level mediated action is producing this action differently and may be focused on the higher-level mediated action but may also mid- or background it in their own mind.

As mentioned in the section on modal density, we are apt to know when another social actor is focused upon a certain action or interaction. But just as we can tell the (displayed) focus of a social actor, we can read more attention levels of another. The reason for this is that we actually see and hear what kinds of chains of lower-level mediated actions a social actor produces when performing a certain action or interaction. Often, social actors engage in several higher-level mediated actions simultaneously, and thus, we read the actions that they perform, and we are able to read how much (inter)actional attention a social actor pays right off of their modal density. While we do this in our everyday lives without really knowing that we do this, we can be systematic in our analysis as researchers and explicate exactly which of the simultaneously produced higher-level mediated actions a social actor pays more and which they pay less attention to. In turn, we can then use the graph (Figure 2.8) and place these higher-level mediated actions relationally to one another on a modal density foreground–background continuum of attention/awareness and thus make the social actor's displayed attention levels apparent.

In the above example, we see that Karen pays more attention to her driving than to her speaking with the children about their homework. But of course, social actors do not continually focus upon the same higher-level mediated action.

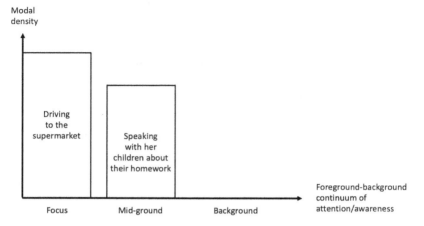

Figure 2.8 Modal density foreground–background continuum of attention/ awareness: example Karen.

Semantic/Pragmatic Means

History

Developed in Norris (2002a), first published in Norris (2004a).

Theory

Since social actors can only produce one focused higher-level mediated action at a time, even though social actors often engage in more than one higher-level mediated action, social actors need to structure their attention levels. They do this interactively by producing a pronounced lower-level mediated action, which is neither part of the previously focused-upon higher-level mediated action, nor a part of the newly focused-upon higher-level mediated action. As social actors thus structure (inter)actional meaning, the *means* presents an aspect of semantics. At the very same time, other social actors read the pronounced lower-level mediated action that a social actor performs as an indication of change in focused upon higher-level mediated action. Others react to the *means*, and the pronounced lower-level mediated action thus presents an aspect of pragmatics.

Analytical Tool

When a social actor is about to change their focused upon higher-level mediated action, they produce a pronounced lower-level mediated action, which has no bearing on the focused upon or the about to be focused-upon higher-level mediated action. The structuring of focus can occur right before the switch or it can occur minutes before the actual refocusing is accomplished. In order to find the semantic/pragmatic means, the analyst first delineates the two higher-level mediated actions. Second, the analyst transcribes the segment, including parts before and after the transition. During transcription, the semantic/pragmatic means becomes apparent.

Examples

Ben, who is married to Zoe, has almost finished cleaning the kitchen and wants to play a computer game. As soon as he *decides* to play the game when he is done with cleaning, he produces an eyebrow raise as a semantic/pragmatic means.

Steve, an accountant, is talking with his secretary and wants to go back to his own office to see a client. As soon as he thinks about going back to his office, he slaps his knee as a semantic/pragmatic means.

Some Analytical Capabilities

1 Discovery of how a social actor structures their focus and thus the higher-level mediated actions in their attention/awareness.
2 Discovery of how other social actors react to the display of an upcoming change in somebody else's focused-upon higher-level mediated action.
3 Discovery that social actors can produce semantic/pragmatic means in order to refocus another's focused-upon higher-level mediated actions.
4 Discovery of various kinds of structuring devices (semantic/pragmatic means).

Social actors always perform higher-level mediated actions. These higher-level mediated actions can be of various scales (see below), but no matter the scale, we can only produce one higher-level mediated action in our focus of attention. Simultaneously, as explicated above, we can produce a number of other higher-level mediated actions that we are not focused upon. In everyday action and interaction, social actors change their focus sometimes quite frequently and sometimes only after a relatively long duration of focusing upon a particular higher-level mediated action. As we refocus, we restructure the meaning in our mind and in order to do so, we produce a pronounced lower-level mediated action that we call a *semantic means*. Often, the semantic means is produced nonverbally through a pronounced eyebrow raise or a hand beat or the like. Sometimes, semantic means can also be a verbal utterance such as OK. Simultaneously, this very same *means* communicates to others that we are about to change our focus. Since the *means* communicates to others in action and interaction, we call it also a *pragmatic means*. Thus, every pronounced lower-level mediated action that indicates a shift in our focused-upon higher-level mediated action and therefore indicates a restructuring in our minds, is called a *semantic/pragmatic means* because of its dual function.

Scales of Action

History

First published in Norris (2009b), clearly developed as analytical tool in Norris (2017b).

Theory

Social actors continuously produce consecutive actions. However, not all consecutive actions are linked. While small scale higher-level mediated actions are always embedded in larger scale higher-level mediated actions, not all small scale higher-level mediated actions belong to the same larger scale higher-level mediated action, when performed consecutively. For example, a social actor can perform five consecutive higher-level mediated actions of which three belong together, and these three are a part of a larger scale higher-level mediated action, while the other two belong to completely different larger scale higher-level mediated actions.

Analytical Tool

When a social actor performs a higher-level mediated action, this action is often linked to other higher-level mediated actions performed. Higher-level mediated actions can be teased apart as to being of a smaller or a larger scale. The analyst first teases apart various higher-level mediated actions, analyzes their various scales and how they are embedded, and then determines to which larger scale higher-level mediated actions they belong.

Example

Karen, who has a catering business, has a school-aged child. One after-noon Karen performs the following higher-level mediated actions:

Karen makes a shopping list.
Karen drives to the supermarket.
Karen speaks with her child about homework.
Karen buys groceries.
Karen drives home.
Karen speaks with her child about homework.
Karen unpacks the car.
Karen puts the groceries away.
Karen helps her child with homework.

Here, we find two larger scale higher-level mediated actions: (1) shopping for groceries (let us imaging Karen has to drive to the store) and (2) helping her child with homework.

While the higher-level mediated actions of speaking with her child about homework are clearly embedded in the higher-level mediated action of driving, the actual larger scale higher-level action is of a different kind than shopping for groceries of which the two drives are an intricate part. Karen could have performed the larger scale higher-level mediated action of shopping without speaking with her child about homework. Similarly, she could have spoken with her child about homework without driving to the grocery store. However, she could not have bought groceries without the drives.

Some Analytical Capabilities

1   Discovery of how social actors consecutively perform higher-level mediated actions that are part of different larger scale higher-level mediated actions.

2   Discovery of how other social actors understand the per-formed higher-level mediated actions as clearly belonging to different larger scale higher-level mediated actions.

3   Discovery that social actors can produce simultaneous higher-level mediated actions belonging to different larger scale higher-level actions.

As social actors go about their everyday lives, they on the one hand perform simultaneous higher-level mediated actions focusing on one action at a time as explained above; and on the other hand, they produce higher-level mediated actions consecutively. A consecutive nature of higher-level mediated actions in everyday life is what we notice most easily: I wash the dishes, make coffee, put laundry into the washing machine, sit down at my laptop and write—all consecutive higher-level mediated actions. One follows the other. It appears logical that we move from point A to point B. However, while we do move from one higher-level mediated action (on whichever level of attention) to another, consecutively (and simultaneously) performed higher-level mediated actions are often a part of different larger scale higher-level mediated actions. Going back to my example above, where I only spoke of consecutively performed higher-level mediated actions, doing the dishes and putting laundry in the washing machine belong to the larger scale higher-level mediated action of doing things around the home. The higher-level mediated action of making coffee, sitting at my laptop and writing in this instance belong to the larger scale higher-level mediated action of writing a book (Figures 2.9 and 2.10).

When looking closely at the various higher-level mediated actions here, we find that making coffee, for example, could also be a part of a different larger scale higher-level mediated action, so could sitting at my laptop and writing. What this shows is that we need to have some

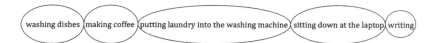

Figure 2.9 Consecutively performed higher-level mediated actions.

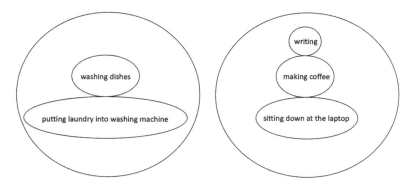

Figure 2.10 Belonging to two different larger scale higher-level mediated actions.

deep understanding of the social actor who is performing the higher-level mediated actions in order to be able to analyze correctly which larger scale higher-level actions they belong to at a particular moment.

When utilizing this analytical tool, we can further tease apart the complexity that exists in everyday life and we can begin to make sense of the micro actions linking them to the larger scale actions that they belong to.

Site of Engagement

History

Developed in Scollon (1998), refined in Norris and Jones (2005) and further refined in Norris (2014, 2019).

Theory

Every concretely performed higher-level mediated action is performed at a site of engagement, which makes the production of the higher-level mediated action possible by linking to at least one (but often more) practice(s) as well as to at least one (but often more) societal discourse(s). Concrete higher-level mediated actions (micro level), practices (meso level) and discourses (macro level) thus come together at a site of engagement. Practices are defined as higher-level mediated actions with a history (Scollon 1998) and discourses are defined as practices with an institutional dimension (Norris 2014).

Analytical Tool

When a social actor produces a (concrete) higher-level mediated action, this higher-level mediated action links to the abstracted level (practice) which incorporates all of those previously (often by other social actors) performed higher-level mediated actions (actions with a history, i.e., meso level). Simultaneously, the (concrete) higher-level mediated action links to societal discourses (those practices that have an institutional dimension, i.e., macro level). Often, we find that some practices and/or discourses converge with the concrete higher-level mediated action, whereas at other times, we find that some practices and/or discourses diverge from the concretely performed higher-level mediated action.

Examples

Ben, who is married to Zoe, is playing a computer game in the same room where Zoe is talking with her parents about family matters. Ben sometimes is addressed and is somewhat engaged in the conversation.

Some Analytical Capabilities

1   Discovery of how a concrete higher-level mediated action is shaped by converging and/or diverging practices.
2   Discovery of how a concrete higher-level mediated action is shaped by converging and/or diverging discourses.
3   Discovery of how several practices and several discourses can be at play when a particular higher-level mediated action is being produced.
4   Discovery of how practices and discourses enforce certain higher-level mediated actions.
5   Discovery of how practices and/or discourses are being shaped and changed by concrete higher-level mediated actions.

The site of engagement is that window opened up through practices and discourses that make the concrete higher-level mediated action possible (Scollon 1998; Norris 2014). When using the site of engagement as an analytical tool, we can take the window-analogy further and think about either closing the window to a narrow slit (thereby only looking at a very small higher-level mediated action), or we can think of opening the window wider to examine a larger aspect of a concrete higher-level mediated action.

No matter how narrow or wide our view on the micro higher-level mediated action, the site of engagement always forces the analyst to bring in the meso (practice) level and the macro (discourse) level. Thus, the concept of a site of engagement makes clear that we can never just get stuck at one level, be that the micro (concrete higher-level mediated action), the meso (practice) or the macro (discourse) level.

When we take the example above, we can draw a diagram that illustrates how the concrete higher-level mediated action of Ben playing a computer game in the room where Zoe is speaking with her parents about family matters is impacted by practices and discourses (Figure 2.11).

Here, at this site of engagement, we see that Ben is playing a computer game and is also somewhat engaged in the conversation with Zoe and her parents. Here, gaming practice and the practice of having family

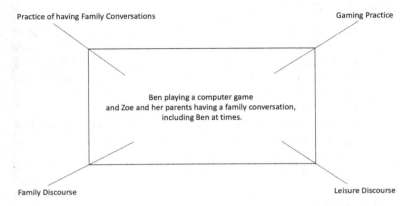

Practice of having Family Conversations

Gaming Practice

Ben playing a computer game
and Zoe and her parents having a family conversation,
including Ben at times.

Family Discourse

Leisure Discourse

Figure 2.11 Site of engagement of Ben playing a computer game and simultaneously interacting with Zoe and her parents in a family conversation.

conversations intersect with the concretely performed higher-level mediated actions. Further, we see that the family discourse and the leisure discourse intersect.

Time Cycles and (Inter)action Rhythms

History

Time cycles in relation to mediated actions developed by Scollon (2005), linking interaction rhythms and their relationship to time cycles developed and first published in Norris (2017a).

Theory

Scollon (2005: 24, italics original) demonstrated how mediated actions are entrained to at least six different (but integral) pace makers (*Zeitgeber*):

- *The cardiac-respiratory cycle*: pulsation of the heart and of breathing
- *The metabolic cycle*: ebbs and flow of ingestion, digestion and elimination, pain cycles, drowsiness cycles
- *The circadian cycle*: 24-hour revolution of the earth about its axis
- *The lunar cycle*: 28-day revolution of the moon around the earth
- *The solar cycle*: 365-day revolution of the earth around the sun
- *Entropic cycles*: formation and decay of material substances

In Norris (2017a) it is demonstrated:

- How both the circadian and the solar cycles in international family video conferences were doubled (due to the fact that the participants were situated in different parts of the world with one being in the Southern and one being in the Northern Hemisphere, each with a different day-time and a different season)
- That (inter)action rhythms (day-rhythms as well rhythms of an intermediate and of a large order) impact:
  - the video conference (inter)action
  - the participants' conception of time

Analytical Tool

Time cycles and (inter)action rhythms allow to

- examine lived and understood time
- gain an expanded view beyond a clock-time re-construction of concrete (inter)actions

Examples

Mary lives in New Zealand. It is early Saturday morning on a summer day when her mother calls from Canada, where it is Friday afternoon on a brisk winter day (i.e., two circadian and two solar cycles).

A mother calls her daughter on Skype and the daughter keeps turning away from the screen to attend to her toddler. In the meantime, the mother continues to chat without interruption (i.e.. mother and daughter have the large (inter)action cycle of mothering in common as the mother remembers what it is like to have a toddler).

Some Analytical Capabilities

1   Discovery of how many time cycles or rhythms social actors entrain to during a particular (inter)action.
2   Discovery of various (inter)action rhythms.

We find rhythms in interaction at many different levels (Erickson 1980; Scollon 1981; Norris 2009b). But the concepts of time cycles and (inter)action rhythms allow us to unpack the complexity of the many cycles that each social actor engaged in the (inter)action is entrained to. When social actors are (inter)acting in the same place, they are

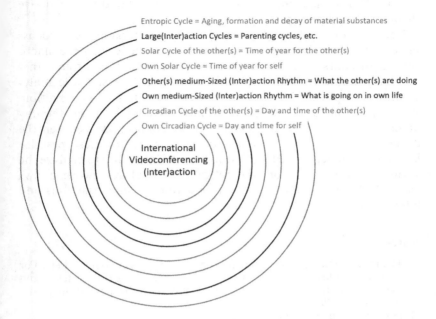

Figure 2.12 Natural experienced time cycles and rhythms (also, but a little differently, shown in Norris 2019: 261).

entrained to the same circadian, lunar and solar cycles. However, when participants (inter)acting are positioned on different sides of the planet, as is the fact when a social actor from New Zealand skypes a social actor in Canada, the cycles no longer overlap.

In a study conducted in New Zealand, I demonstrated this when a daughter in New Zealand skyped her mother in Canada. The many time cycles and (inter)action rhythms that came into play are shown in Figure 2.12.

When examining how concrete higher-level mediated actions are entrenched in natural rhythms and time cycles, we can see how they naturally come together.

Conclusion

This chapter has outlined the history and theory of 12 analytical concepts and their analytical capabilities for the analysis of human action and interaction. By giving examples and drawing connections between the analytical concepts, the chapter demonstrates how the

12 analytical tools comprehensively fit together, building a cohesive theory and methodology.

Rather than simplifying the complexity of (inter)actions by focusing on either the micro level *or* the meso practice level *or* the macro societal discourse level, the framework, with its multiple strongly theoretically grounded analytical tools, allows for the systematic analysis of the complexity that is found in everyday action and interaction. With this possibility of analyzing the inherent complexity in everyday human life, we can begin to draw strong connections between the concrete micro level of actions and interactions, the meso practice level and the macro societal discourse level. The ability to analyze the various levels based on one theoretical/analytical framework, allows us to shed new insight onto the production of human actions and interactions.

Notes

1 The terms "embodiment" and "perception" may come to mind here. For a detailed philosophical and theoretical understanding of these terms and their relationship to the analytical tools discussed throughout this book, see Norris (2019).
2 For a definition of mode, refer to Chapter 1.
3 Of course, there are other higher-level mediated actions in which the mode of touch builds an intricate part and is highly relevant for the higher-level mediated action (such as shaking hands) to unfold socially correctly.
4 For details about multimodal transcription conventions, see Norris (2004a, 2011, or 2019 as well as above).

References

Erickson, F. 1980. Timing and context in children's everyday discourse: Implications for the study of referential and social meaning. *Sociolinguistic Working Paper 67(1–43)*. Austin, TX: Southwestern Educational Development Laboratory.

Lemke, J. 2000a. Across the scales of time: Artifacts, activities, and meanings in ecosocial systems. *Mind, Culture, and Activity*, 7(4), 273–290.

Lemke, J. 2000b. Opening up closure: Semiotics across scales. In: Chandler, J.L.R. and Van de Vijver, G. (eds.) *Closure: Emergent organizations and their dynamics (Annals of the New York Academy of Sciences)*, Vol. 901. New York: New York Academy of Sciences, 100–111.

Norris, S. 2002a. A theoretical framework for multimodal discourse analysis presented via the analysis of identity construction of two women living in Germany. Department of Linguistics: Georgetown University. Dissertation: UMI.

Norris, S. 2002b. The implication of visual research for discourse analysis: Transcription beyond language. *Visual Communication* 1(1), 97–121.

Norris, S. 2004a. *Analyzing multimodal interaction: A methodological framework.* London: Routledge.

Norris, S. 2004b. Multimodal discourse analysis: A conceptual framework. In: Levine, P. and Scollon, R. (eds.) *Discourse and technology: Multimodal discourse analysis.* Washington, DC: Georgetown University Press, 101–115.

Norris, S. 2005. Habitus, social identity, the perception of male domination – And agency? In: Norris, Sigrid and Jones, R. (eds.) *Discourse in action: Introducing mediated discourse analysis.* London: Routledge, 183–197.

Norris, S. 2006. Multiparty interaction: A multimodal perspective on relevance. *Discourse Studies* 8(3), 401–421.

Norris, S. 2009a. Modal density and modal configurations: Multimodal actions. In Jewit, C. (ed.) *Routledge handbook for multimodal discourse analysis.* London: Routledge.

Norris, S. 2009b. Tempo, *Auftakt*, Levels of actions, and practice: Rhythms in ordinary interactions. *Journal of Applied Linguistics* 6(3), 333–356.

Norris, S. 2011. *Identity in (inter)action: Introducing multimodal (inter)action analysis.* Berlin and Boston, MA: deGruyter Mouton.

Norris, S. 2013. What is a mode? Smell, olfactory perception, and the notion of mode in multimodal mediated theory. *Multimodal Communication* 2(2), 155–169.

Norris, S. 2014. The impact of literacy based schooling on learning a creative practice: Modal configurations, practices and discourses. *Multimodal Communication* 3(2), 181–195.

Norris, S. 2017a. Rhythmus und Resonanz in internationalen Videokonferenzen. In: Breyer, T., Buchholz, M., Hamburger, A., and Pfänder, S. (eds.) *Resonanz, Rhythmus & Synchronisierung: Erscheinungsformen und Effekte.* Bielefeld: transcript-Verlag.

Norris, S. 2017b. Scales of action: An example of driving & car talk in Germany and North America. *Text & Talk* 37(1), 117–139.

Norris, S. 2019. *Systematically working with multimodal data: Research methods in multimodal discourse analysis.* Hoboken, NJ: Wiley Blackwell.

Norris, S. and Jones, R.H. 2005. *Discourse in action: Introducing mediated discourse analysis.* London: Routledge.

Pirini, J. April 2016. Intersubjectivity and materiality: A multimodal perspective. *Multimodal Communication* 5(1), 1–14.

Scollon, R. 1981. *Tempo, density, and DSiklence: Rhythm in ordinary talk.* Fairbanks, AK: Centre for Cross-Cultural Studies, University of Alaska.

Scollon, R. 1998. *Mediated discourse as social interaction: A study of news discourse.* London: Longman.

Scollon, R. 2001. *Mediated discourse: The nexus of practice*. London: Routledge.

Vygotsky, L.S. 1978 *Mind in society: The development of higher psychological processes*, eds. M. Cole, V. John-Steiner, S. Scribner, and E. Souberman. Cambridge, MA: Harvard University Press.

Wertsch, J.V. 1998. *Voices of the mind: A sociocultural approach to mediated action*. Cambridge, MA: Harvard University Press.

3 Examining Multimodal Identity

Theory and Analytical Tools

Introduction

Chapter 1 explicated the overarching notions of the framework, outlining multimodal (inter)action analysis, (inter)action, (inter)actional attention, mediation and mode. Chapter 2 moved deeper into analytical tools for the analysis of actions and interactions and this chapter outlines the analytical tools and their theoretical notions for the analysis of identity. But upfront, a note that in multimodal discourse analysis we work in a systematic way as outlined in Norris (2019). This way of working is not replicated in this book. Rather, the chapters in this book focus in greater detail upon the theoretical and analytical concepts and tools explicated within. In many ways, it may be useful for the interested researcher to use the two books in tandem because the information is not replicated. In Norris (2019) some of the analytical tools that are discussed in this chapter are discussed from a different vantage point. However, there I only very briefly describe how those tools are useful for the analysis of identity.

This chapter briefly and clearly explicates 16 concepts to analyze identity, listing for each in a gray textbox:

1 The history of the concept, that is, when and where it was developed and when and where it was first (or most clearly) published. Based on this information, the reader can then go to the reference list and find detailed bibliographical information on both.
2 The theory that is embedded in the concept.
3 How the concept is used as an analytical tool to analyze data.
4 Brief practical example(s), elucidating the concept.
5 Some analytical capabilities of the concept.

The text that follows each textbox of concise information goes into more detail about the concept, adding a longer example and/or an image and/or a graph to illustrate the concept further. Examples, some real and some envisioned, are used throughout merely to enhance comprehension of the analytical tools.

The chapter is brief and can be used as a guide for how to analyze everyday identity production. The data may be video and audio recordings of social actors acting and interacting, or content from the Internet, movies, TV and so on. For possible data collection and a systematic way to analyze the data, refer to Norris (2019) because such a discussion is outside the scope of this chapter. The aim of the chapter is to explicate the theoretical and analytical bases of the tools that can be used to analyze everyday identity production.

Necessary Theoretical Background

The analytical tools discussed below build upon the following notions:

- All actions are mediated actions (Vygotsky 1978; Scollon 1998, 2001; Wertsch 1998). A mediated action is defined by Wertsch and Scollon as social actors acting with or through mediational means/ cultural tools. Discussions of mediated actions in relation to the analytical tools explicated in this book can be found in Norris and Jones (2005) and Norris (2004a, 2011, 2019).
- A mode is defined as a system of mediated action (Norris 2013; Chapter 1 of this book).

Each mediated action is identity-telling (Scollon 1997).

Identity

Identity is fluid, ever changing, developing and analyzable as situated in action and interaction. Two primary concepts will set the stage for this chapter: The concept of social-time-place and the concept of identity elements. After having discussed these two concepts, I shall move on to the lower-level, the higher-level and frozen mediated actions and discuss how they are useful analytical tools by themselves to shed light on identity production in (inter)action. Once these concepts are covered, I discuss modal configurations, which is an analytical tool that is used for microanalysis of concretely produced identity elements. With these analytical tools discussed, I move on to aspects of horizontal identity production, which takes the previously discussed notions of the various mediated actions as a prerequisite. In order to explicate the concept of horizontal identity production, the three analytical tools of modal density, the modal density foreground–background continuum and semantic/pragmatic means, are needed. I first illustrate how each of these is used separately, before I show how they come together. After horizontal identity production has been explicated, I delve into vertical identity production. Here, again several concepts, from immediate identity element production and the central layer of discourse, continuous identity element production and the intermediary layer of discourse, as well as general identity element production and the outer layers of discourse, are needed. Here too, I first explicate each of these analytical tools separately, before I show how they all come together. Then, I cover the analytical tool scales of action, which allows us to see a bigger picture of where and how particular identity elements are produced; and as the last analytical tool discussed in this chapter, I illuminate how we can use the site of engagement to shed even larger insight upon identity element production, bridging micro, meso and macro levels.

Social-Time-Place

History

Developed in Norris (2002), first published in Norris (2011).

Theory

Identity is conceived of as being produced in connection with social others, during a particular time in history, and at a particular place.

Analytical Tool

Every social actor produces mediated actions with other social actors and with or through multiple mediational means/cultural tools available at the particular time and place in which the actions occur, producing particular identity elements. By examining the social-time-place in which social actors produce their identity elements, we gain insight into the social, historical and place-situatedness of identity.

Examples

1   A mother is a stay-at-home mother.
2   A mother is a working mother.

Analytical Capability

1   Discovery of how a specific identity element is produced at a specific social-time-place.

Identity Elements

History

Developed in Norris (2002), first published in Norris (2007), and more thoroughly explained in Norris (2011).

Theory

Identity is conceived of as a constantly developing process. Identity elements are flexible and of heuristic value as it allows us to analyze how some identity elements are short-lived, while others are more durable. But even the durable identity elements are fluid in their makeup as is evident when analyzing mediated actions and how they produce identity.

Analytical Tool

Every mediated action that a social actor performs produces an identity element. Usually, social actors produce more than one higher-level mediated action, thereby producing several identity elements simultaneously (as will be discussed in detail below).

Examples

1   I am writing this book, producing my author identity element.
2   My dogs are sleeping close to my desk, producing my dog-owner identity element.
3   My partner is making dinner and conversing with me, producing my partner identity element.

Some Analytical Capabilities

1   Discovery of a great variety of identity elements that we are producing on our own and with others (even with our dogs).
2   Discovery of the simultaneity of identity element production (see "Horizontal Identity Production" below).
3   Discovery of various layers of concretely produced identity elements (see "Vertical Identity Production" below).

Social-time-place and identity element production in action and interaction go hand-in-hand since we are always interested in the situated nature of identity, we are interested in the historical positioning of identity and we are interested in how and through which mediational means/cultural tools particular identity elements are produced. A study of identity is not limited to the study of social actors in their everyday lives. Rather, we can use the framework and its concepts to examine identity production in TV, movies, YouTube and much more.

While social-time-place and identity element production are indeed our larger interest, the concepts detailed below are the ones that allow us to analyze the identity elements that social actors produce at any given social-time-place.

Because all analytical tools are theoretically interconnected, I begin with the smallest unit of analysis—the (inter)actional meaning unit, the lower-level mediated action.

Lower-level Mediated Action

History

Developed in Norris (2002), first published in relation to identity in Norris (2005), but most clearly published in relation to identity in Norris (2011).

Theory

The lower-level mediated action is the smallest *(inter)actional meaning unit* that a social actor uses and is able to read in interaction. Always mediated in multiple ways. Each lower-level mediated action tells of identity.

Analytical Tool

A single social actor produces a lower-level mediated action with or through multiple mediational means/cultural tools. The way the social actor produces the lower-level mediated action by using particular mediational means or cultural tools allows us to gain insight into the social actor's identity.

Examples

1 Peter says *"howdy."*
2 Laura *smiles* at a puppy.
3 Mary *tosses a coin* into a homeless person's hat.

Some Analytical Capabilities

1 Discovery of how a specific lower-level mediated action (or chains thereof) can tell us something about the identity of a social actor.
2 Discovery of mediational means/cultural tools used in the production of a specific identity-telling lower-level mediated action.

The lower-level mediated action was developed and linked to identity in Norris (2002). From 2005 onward, it appears in publications related to identity, but is most clearly outlined in regards to identity production in Norris (2011). The lower-level mediated action is defined as the smallest (inter)actional (or pragmatic) meaning unit of a mode with a beginning and an end. Examples of a mode are language, gesture, gaze, posture, proxemics or walking. Chapter 1 already introduced the concepts of mode and mediated action, and the definition is given also above. As explained in detail in Chapter 2, just as all other mediated actions, the lower-level mediated action always consists of social actor(s) acting with or through multiple mediational means/cultural tools. Each lower-level mediated action builds chains in an interaction, which intersect with other chains. In this way, lower-level mediated actions are identity-telling. The notion of mediation was not always emphasized (Norris 2002, 2004a,b, 2005, 2007) because no action can be accomplished without being mediated. However, more recently (Norris 2017a,b, 2019), the term "mediated" is being emphasized much stronger because we can learn much about identity production by analyzing in which ways lower-level actions are mediated. The mediational means/cultural tools used give much insight into particular identity elements that social actors produce.

When examining how a person produces their identity element of a research participant, we can examine the lower-level actions and chains thereof that the participant produces. Figure 3.1 illustrates a research participant as he touches the research laptop's mouse pad (a lower-level mediated action).

Here, the lower-level action is mediated by the participant's hand, by the research laptop, as well as the desk, etc. It is particularly the mediational means that give away which identity element is being produced. Was he instead using his own laptop, he could be performing the seemingly exact same lower-level mediated action of touching a mouse pad, yet, the lower-level action would be a different one especially because it would be mediated by different cultural tools. Thus, when examining the identity elements that are being produced, a close

Figure 3.1 Lower-level mediated action of touching the mousepad: production of an aspect of a participant identity element.

look at the cultural tools that are mediating the lower-level actions and their chains, gives us insight into identity production. But, of course, no lower-level mediated action (or chain of lower-level mediated action) is ever produced alone. Rather, we always find a multitude of such chains coming together and intersecting in various ways at various points in (inter)action, as they are produced by and simultaneously produce higher-level mediated actions.

Higher-level Mediated Action

History

Developed in Norris (2002), first published in in relation to identity in Norris (2005), and clearly explicated in relation to identity in Norris (2007, 2011).

Theory

The coming together of multiple chains of lower-level mediated actions build a higher-level mediated action. Simultaneously, the higher-level mediated action that social actors produce builds the multiple chains of lower-level mediated actions. Higher- and lower-level mediated actions thus co-produce each other in interaction.

Each higher-level mediated action is identity-telling.

Analytical Tool

A single social actor produces a higher-level mediated action through the coming together of multiple chains of lower-level mediated actions. No two people produce a co-constructed higher-level mediated action through the exact same chaining of lower-level mediated actions. In this way, each social actor produces their very own identity element through the production of the higher-level mediated action.

Examples

Peter and Mary are having dinner. Peter serves Mary her food and Mary silently nods.

Gary is mowing the lawn as he is singing.

A person, even if not or only partially visible, is explaining something in a YouTube clip in a happy tone of voice.

Some Analytical Capabilities

1   Discovery of which chains of lower-level mediated actions are used by each participant in the production of a specific higher-level mediated action and how these chains of lower-level mediated actions tell of their identity elements.

2   Discovery of how the higher-level mediated actions produced by each social actor involved come together in co-produced interactions, strengthening or weakening particular aspects of the social actors' identity elements.

3 Discovery of how social actors pay more or less attention to several higher-level mediated actions at a time and thereby produce several identity elements simultaneously.

4 Discovery of how focused-upon higher-level mediated actions are shared or not shared in co-produced interaction and what kind of identity elements are produced in the focus, mid-ground or background of attention/awareness by each social actor.

5 Discovery of the modal density of specific higher-level mediated actions for each social actor involved in a co-produced interaction and how the modal density tells of identity.

6 Discovery of the modal configurations produced by each social actor in a co-produced interaction and how modal configurations tell of identity.

7 Discovery that each social actor on their own can and does produce higher-level mediated actions when interacting with the environment or objects and discovery of how the social actor thus produces their particular identity elements.

More often than not, we are interested in the higher-level mediated actions that social actors produce since it is through higher-level mediated actions that social actors produce identity elements. When we revisit the example above (Figure 3.1), we see that the participant is sitting in a research space and that he is surrounded by cameras and an audio recording device. Here, we see multiple chains of lower-level mediated actions coming together, all together building the participant identity element that the social actor is producing at this moment. As discussed in detail in Norris (2007), some identity elements are fleeting (such as the participant identity element), while others are more durable (such as a social actor's gender identity element). Was the social actor (Figure 3.1), however, sitting in a different space without cameras and audio recorder, etc., he could, as mentioned above, produce the seemingly same chains of lower-level action, while he was producing a different higher-level mediated action (working or studying, for example), and thereby producing a different identity element.

What is important is that we need to have quite a bit of background knowledge about the social actors that we study in order to be able to name (1) the actual higher-level mediated action that the social actor produces and (2) the identity element that the social actor produces. These two productions—the production of a higher-level mediated action and the production of an identity element—go hand-in-hand. Neither is prior to the other. However, it is noteworthy that social actors usually consciously produce the higher-level mediated action, while they are not as conscious (or not conscious at all) of the identity element that they are producing. At the same time, we need to realize that others often quickly assign identity elements (fitting or not) to particular higher-level mediated actions. This is something to be aware of, because as researchers we want to be careful to first correctly analyze the higher-level mediated action as it is being produced by a particular social actor through the chains of intersecting lower-level mediated actions. Only then do we want to analyze the identity element that is being produced. It is always the action that allows for the analysis of identity. It is (usually) not the identity element that allows us to gain insight into the higher-level mediated action in everyday life. Rather, it (usually) is the higher-level mediated action that gives insight into identity element production in everyday life. Thus, in everyday life, we want to ask: what is the action that is going on here? And then we want to ask: which identity element is being produced through this action?

This may be different when we examine TV series or movies. There, it is (often) the identity that the performer is trying to (re)present that then leads to the production of particular higher-level mediated actions. Thus, when analyzing movies, we may want to ask: which identity element is being produced here? And then ask: through which action is this identity element being produced in the movie? But, if we do not know the identity element that is supposedly being produced from the outset, we can analyze social actors in movies just as we analyze social actors in real life and move in analysis from action to identity element production.

Frozen Mediated Action

History

Developed in Norris (2002), first published in Norris (2004a).

Theory

As humans we understand the world around us as acted upon by social actors. Therefore, lower-level mediated actions and higher-level mediated actions are embedded in the environment and in objects. The environment and objects are identity-telling.

Analytical Tool

A single lower-level mediated action (such as a brush stroke in a painting) and higher-level mediated action (such as a picture having been placed in a specific spot on a wall) are entailed in the painting itself. The brush stroke, the picture, as well as the place that has been chosen to hang the picture, are identity-telling.

Examples

A brush stroke is frozen (embedded) in the painting itself and *tells us about the identity of the painter.*

A painting is hung up in a specific spot and *tells us of the identity of the social actor who placed the painting there and/or the social actor who resides in the space or owns it.*

Some Analytical Capabilities

1　Discovery of how social actors read mediated actions off of objects and/or the environment as identity-telling.
2　Discovery of which lower-level or higher-level mediated actions are entailed foremost and of whose identity they tell; and which lower- or higher-level mediated actions are entailed in a more hidden way and of whose identity they tell.
3　Discovery of how the identity-telling frozen mediated actions are mediated in multiple ways and how the mediational means/cultural tools within the frozen actions tell of identity.

The frozen actions entailed in the cameras and the audio recorder standing on the desk in the research space, in which the participant is taking part in a study illustrated in Figure 3.1, are identity-telling of the researchers as well as of the participant. So are the research laptop, the desk in its position, etc. All of these objects and the way the environment is set up are identity-telling as they embed the previously produced mediated actions of: (1) setting up the room (by the researchers) and (2) (the participant) having sat down and moved the chair to the position where the participant is now sitting in the research space. When realizing that the environment and objects embed mediated actions that some social actors (here the researchers and the participant) produced at an earlier time, we can learn to understand how previously performed mediated actions are also identity-telling (Norris 2011; Norris and Makboon 2015).

However, as with higher- and lower-level mediated actions, we need to have much background knowledge of the social actors that we are studying (and those that are involved in our study as the researchers themselves) in order to be able to correctly analyze the identity elements of which the frozen mediated actions speak.

Modal Configuration and Modal Aggregates

History

First published in Norris (2009a). First used to analyze identity in Norris (2014b).

Theory

Modal configuration is the hierarchical ordering of lower-level mediated actions in (often small scale) higher-level mediated actions. This means that some modes are of more and some modes are of less importance for the higher-level mediated action to unfold as it does. The particular use of modal configurations is identity-telling.

A modal aggregate is the fusion of two or more lower-level mediated actions (or chains thereof) on the same hierarchical level.

Analytical Tool

A social actor produces certain modal configurations (sometimes including modal aggregates) in (inter)action when producing higher-level mediated actions. Modal configurations can change quickly, making it often important to examine small scale higher-level mediated actions to determine which identity elements they tell of.

Examples

When Ken is speaking on his mobile with high modal density while his partner is waiting, the mode of mobile phone use and the mode of language build a modal aggregate and take on the hierarchically superior position since without the mobile phone or language, the conversation would not unfold as it does. But other modes that sit in a subordinate position on this hierarchical scale, come into play that tell us of how Ken produces his work-identity element in relation to his partner identity element. Here, we would look at how he positions his body (mode of posture), how far away or close he positions himself in relation to his partner (mode of proxemics), etc.

When Zoe is happily knitting the sweater, object handling is of great hierarchical importance. But here, the modes of written language and the images that direct her in how to knit the intricate pattern build a modal aggregate with object handling since neither knitting alone, nor reading the pattern alone would allow her to produce the actions that she produces. But other modes also come into play. We can see in Zoe's facial expression how happy she is and can read in her posture how relaxed she is, and so on. All of these modes (or chains of lower-level mediated actions) can give us insight into her identity element production of a knitter. Here, we can see how strongly or weakly developed the identity element is and so on.

Some Analytical Capabilities

1. Discovery of hierarchies of lower-level mediated actions and their chains and how they tell of identity.
2. Discovery of modal aggregates (i.e., modes that necessarily have to be produced together and that are intertwined to the extent that the meaning of the mediated action cannot be understood without them building an aggregate). The correct production of modal aggregates can give insight into the strength (the level of mastery or appropriation) of an identity element.
3. Discovery of how specific modal configurations display the knowledge of a social actor and with it the strength (the level of mastery or appropriation) of an identity element.
4. Discovery of where the mode of language (or any other mode) actually sits in hierarchical terms within a specific higher-level action and to what extent the mode of language (or any other mode) actually tells about specific identity elements in relation to other modes.

Modal configurations and the production (or nonproduction) of modal aggregates, as shown in Norris (2014a,b), can give insight into the level of knowledge of a specific higher-level mediated action and with it the knowledge about the production of a particular identity element. For example, an artist produces particular modal aggregates and particular modal configurations when looking at a painting, whereas an art student may misread the produced modal aggregate and modal configuration of the artist (Norris 2014a,b). Modal configurations and the production of modal aggregates thus produce the teacher's artist identity element, while the incorrect production shows that the art student is not (yet) able to produce an artist identity element. Thus, the fusion of (chains of) lower-level mediated actions, modal aggregates and modal hierarchies (modal configurations) produced in (inter)action can tell much about how higher-level mediated actions, and thus identity elements, are produced and can tell much about the mastery or appropriation of the higher-level mediated actions and identity elements.

Horizontal Identity Production

In order to analyze the simultaneity of identity element production, we need three interlinked concepts: (1) modal density, (2) The modal density foreground–background continuum of attention/awareness and (3) semantic/pragmatic means.

Modal Density

History

Developed in Norris (2002), first published in Norris (2004a), first published in connection with identity in Norris (2007) but more clearly explained in regard to identity in Norris (2011).

Theory

The coming together of chained lower-level mediated actions builds various types of density when a social actor performs a particular higher-level mediated action. Modal density is a short form for lower-level mediated action density. Modal density that a social actor uses to produce a certain higher-level mediated action tells of the amount of attention that they pay to a particular action, and thus to a particular identity element.

Analytical Tool

When a social actor performs a higher-level mediated action, modal density can be analyzed as either being of intensity or of complexity through interconnectedness of chains of lower-level mediated actions, or both. Modal density of a particular higher-level mediated action becomes apparent once the analyst has successfully delineated the higher-level action from others being performed and becomes clearly identifiable during multimodal transcription.[1]

Modal density is one tool that is used in connection with the foreground–background continuum of attention/awareness, building the modal density foreground–background continuum. For clarity, first modal density and then the continuum are explained here.

Examples

Ken is speaking with his coworker about an important topic on his mobile, producing a coworker identity element, while his partner is waiting for him. He is thus simultaneously producing a partner identity element. Each of these higher-level mediated actions and their produced identity elements are created through different modal density.

Some Analytical Capabilities

1   Discovery of the weight of various modes (or better chains of lower-level mediated action) in the performance of a particular higher-level mediated action and how these produce a particular identity element.

2   Discovery of how the lower-level mediated actions chain together as they are producing/being produced by the particular higher-level mediated action, displaying a particular identity element with a certain modal density.

3   Discovery of the ways in which chains of lower-level mediated actions actually build an intricate and sometimes even a most important part in the higher-level mediated action and have great importance in the production of a social actor's identity element.

4   Discovery of the fact that social actors often produce several simultaneous higher-level mediated actions with different amounts of modal density. Each tell of identity elements of the social actor(s) and can be placed on a continuum of attention/awareness levels (see "Modal Density Foreground–Background Continuum of Attention/Awareness" below).

Modal Density Foreground–Background Continuum of Attention/Awareness

History

Developed in Norris (2002), first published in Norris (2004a), first published as linked to identity in Norris (2007), explained in great detail in regard to identity in Norris (2011).

Theory

Social actors often produce more than one higher-level mediated action, even though only one focused higher-level mediated action can be produced at a time. All of these simultaneously produced higher-level mediated actions tell of the social actor's identity elements.

A higher-level mediated action produced by a social actor through high modal density, in relation to other higher-level mediated actions performed simultaneously, displays the social actor's focus on the action and the identity element. The less attention a social actor pays to a certain higher-level mediated action, the lower the modal density that they display in regard to the actions and the identity elements.

Simultaneously performed higher-level mediated actions and/or the identity elements that they produce can be placed on a heuristic foreground–background continuum of attention/awareness.

Analytical Tool

When a social actor performs several higher-level mediated actions at the same time, social actors also (often) produce different identity elements at the very same time. Modal density of each higher-level mediated action can be analyzed, which gives us insight into how much attention a social actor pays to the produced identity element.

First, the analyst realizes the various higher-level mediated actions as distinct from one another, each producing a (different or same) identity element. Then, the analyst discovers the modal intensity or complexity or both during multimodal transcription. Once modal density of all higher-level mediated actions and their produced identity elements are discovered, the analyst utilizes the heuristic and places the simultaneously performed higher-level mediated actions or their corresponding identity elements relationally on the foreground–background continuum of attention/awareness. The identity elements that are produced again and again (over a period of time) on any level of attention/awareness are (often) particularly salient for the social actor. While other higher-level mediated actions and the produced identity elements, even when produced in the focus of attention/awareness that only occur rarely are (usually) of less importance in the social actor's overall identity.

Examples

Laurence is reading the newspaper and is talking to his partner about her day. Laurence rarely reads the paper but speaks every day with his partner about her day.

Karen is driving to the supermarket to buy groceries and talks with her children about their homework. Karen usually helps her children with homework, and she is usually the one buying groceries.

Some Analytical Capabilities

1   Discovery of social actors producing several higher-level mediated actions at a time, all of which also produce the social actor's identity elements.
2   Discovery of how social actors produce various modal densities in the performance of various simultaneously produced higher-level mediated actions, illustrating the attention/awareness levels for each action and the produced identity element.
3   Discovery that social actors in a co-produced higher-level mediated action may not produce the action at the same level of attention/awareness and may produce different identity elements from one another.
4   Discovery of the fact that social actors when paying different levels of attention to the same higher-level mediated action may communicate well without focusing on the same higher-level mediated action and thus without focusing on the same identity element.

Semantic/Pragmatic Means

History

Developed in Norris (2002), first published in Norris (2004a), first published in connection with identity in Norris (2008).

Theory

Since social actors can only produce one focused higher-level mediated action and one identity element at a time, even though social actors often engage in more than one higher-level mediated action and identity element, social actors need to structure their attention levels. They do this (inter)actively by producing a pronounced lower-level mediated action, which neither is part of the previously focused-upon higher-level mediated action and the produced identity element, nor is it part of the newly focused-upon higher-level mediated action and the produced identity element. As social actors thus structure (inter)actional meaning, including the shift from producing one identity element to another in their focus, the means presents an aspect of semantics. At the very same time, other social actors read the pronounced lower-level mediated action that a social actor performs as their change in focused to a different higher-level mediated action and focused upon identity element. Others react to the means, and thus, the pronounced lower-level mediated action presents an aspect of pragmatics.

Analytical Tool

When a social actor is about to change their focus to a different higher-level mediated action and with it change their focus to a different identity element (or a different aspect of the same identity element), they produce a pronounced lower-level mediated action that has no bearing on the focused upon or the about to be focused-upon higher-level mediated actions and the produced identity elements. The structuring of focus can occur right before the switch or it can occur minutes before the actual refocusing is accomplished. In order to find the semantic/pragmatic means, the analyst first delineates the two higher-level mediated actions and the produced identity elements. Second, the analyst transcribes the segment, including parts before and after the transition. During transcription, the semantic/pragmatic means becomes apparent.

Examples

Ben, who is married to Zoe, has almost finished cleaning the kitchen and wants to play a computer game. As soon as he *decides* to play the game when he is done with cleaning, he produces an eyebrow raise.

A change in focused identity element from partner to gamer becomes apparent with the eyebrow raise.

Steve, an accountant, is talking with his secretary and wants to go back to his own office to see a client. As soon as he *thinks about* going back to his office, he slaps his knee.

A change in focused identity element from office superior to the client's accountant becomes apparent with the beat of slapping his knee.

Some Analytical Capabilities

1   Discovery of how social actors structure higher-level mediated actions and their produced identity elements in their attention/awareness levels.

2   Discovery of how other social actors react to the display of an upcoming change in somebody else's focused-upon higher-level mediated action and with it a change in the produced identity element.

3   Discovery that social actors can produce semantic/pragmatic means in order to refocus another's focused-upon higher-level mediated action and with it change others' production of an identity element.

Modal density is a concept that allows for the analysis of the modal intricacies and weighting of a higher-level mediated action and thereby of the produced identity element in a social actor's phenomenally displayed mind. When a social actor produces a higher-level mediated action and with it an identity element, the social actor pays particular attention to it. By placing identity elements relationally onto a modal density foreground–background continuum of attention/awareness (Figure 3.2), a researcher can (1) illustrate the analysis of the modal density (through which the various higher-level mediated actions and identity elements have been produced) and (2) illustrate the relational positioning regarding attention and awareness that a social actor pays to various simultaneously produced identity elements.

When producing graphs as shown in Figure 3.2 for moments in (inter)action over a period of time, the researcher can then see, for example, what kind of identity elements a particular social actor produces again and again. These identity elements may be particularly salient for the social actor during the time of your study.

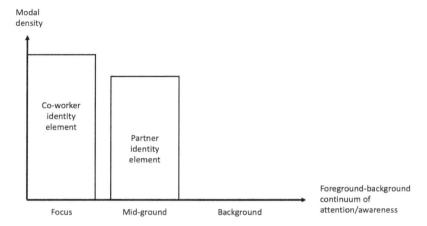

Figure 3.2 Ken is focused upon speaking with his coworker, producing a coworker identity element in the focus, while his partner is waiting
for him, and he is producing a partner identity element in the mid-
ground of his attention/awareness.

Identity element production can sometimes rapidly change within the
attention levels of the performer, whereas at other times, identity elements remain in the attention levels for relatively long periods of time
arranged in the same way. Further, social actors performing an (inter)
action together, often do not focus upon the same higher-level mediated
action, and are thereby often not producing the same identity element
in their focus. The same is true for mid- and backgrounded identity elements. Thus, even when social actors are producing an action together,
their attention levels are not necessarily, and actually, often are not the
same. An example of this is given in Figure 3.3: a mother is shopping for
a catering event and speaking with her child about her homework, displaying her caterer identity element in the focus and her mother identity
element in the mid-ground. Whereas her daughter is focusing on explaining to her mother what parts of her homework she needs her mother's
help with and helping her mother shop, displaying a student identity element in her focus and a daughter identity element in her mid-ground.

Figure 3.3 illustrates the difference in the mother's and the daughter's identity element production in their (inter)action. But once the
shopping is pretty much completed and they are walking toward the
register, the mother produces an eyebrow raise and shifts her attention
to her daughter. Then, her daughter produces a hand beat on the shopping cart and shifts her focus to her mother. Now, identity elements of
the mother and daughter coalesce as shown in Figure 3.4.

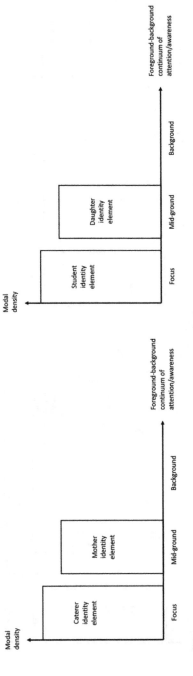

Figure 3.3 Different identity element production in a co-produced interaction.

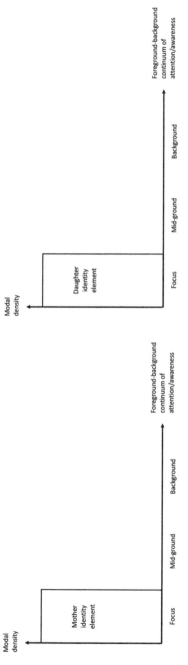

Figure 3.4 Mother and daughter identity elements coalesce.

Now, as they are standing in line at the cash register, the mother puts her arm around her daughter, and they are happily chatting about something, patiently waiting. The previously performed eyebrow raise was a semantic / pragmatic means that indicated the mother's shift in attention from shopping and her caterer identity element to paying focused attention to her daughter and her mother identity element, while the daughter's performed hand beat was the semantic / pragmatic means, indicating her shift in attention.

Vertical Identity Production

In order to analyze vertical identity production, we want to understand three concepts: (1) immediate identity element production and the concrete layer of discourse, (2) continuous identity element production and the (concrete) intermediary layer of discourse and (3) general identity element production and the (concrete) outer layer of discourse.

Immediate Identity Element Production

History

Developed in Norris (2002), first published in Norris (2011).

Theory

Social actors produce concrete higher-level mediated actions, thereby producing identity elements. These concrete higher-level mediated actions with their identity elements build the social actor's central layer of discourse. In this central layer of discourse, the social actor's agency is relatively high.

Analytical Tool

The immediate identity element is an analytical tool that showcases how a social actor produces identity elements in the moment of performing actions or interaction.

Example

Leah writes an essay for her high school history class. As Leah writes her assignment, she produces her immediate student identity element.

Some Analytical Capabilities

1   Discovery of how an immediate identity element is produced.
2   Discovery of how much agency a social actor has when producing an immediate identity element.

Social actors with their habitus and the mediated actions that they are used to performing in their social-time-places or those that they are newly learning all produce a social actor's identity in the immediate sense.

(Norris 2011: 194)

Immediate identity element production is that identity element that a social actor produces as they are performing an action or interaction. In order to illustrate this more clearly, I continue with the example mentioned in the textbox above of Leah writing an essay for her high school history class.

When Leah writes her assignment, she produces her immediate student identity element. Just how Leah performs the action depends upon her. She may listen to music while she is writing the assignment, she may eat a snack and have some tea as she is working on her assignment and so forth. Here, it appears that Leah has quite a bit of agency, even though we of course know that exactly how she produces these actions are deeply embedded in her historical body (Scollon 1998, 2001; Norris 2019). However, as far as agency in higher-level mediated actions is concerned, this concrete level of performing the higher-level mediated action of writing her essay and the thereby created immediate identity element leaves room for agency. But, of course, this is only one small part of producing this concrete mediated action. Next, we want to look at what else is at play.

Continuous Identity Element Production

History

Developed in Norris (2002), first published in Norris (2011).

Theory

Social actors produce concrete higher-level mediated actions and thereby produce identity elements, which are concretely linked to the social actor's network(s). This concrete network-link builds an intermediary layer of discourse. The intermediary layer of discourse constrains the social actor's agency to some extent.

Analytical Tool

The continuous identity element is an analytical tool that showcases that a concrete higher-level mediated action and thereby produced identity element is concretely linked to the social actor's network(s). At this intermediary layer of discourse, network pressures and acceptances between various networks that all concretely link to the concrete mediated action and identity element performed can differ. Thus, one and the same concretely produced mediated action and identity element can be accepted by one concrete network but may be rejected by another concrete network that the social actor belongs to. Thus, we may find incongruity in the intermediary layer of discourse.

Example

Leah writes an essay for her high school history class. Leah's writing of her assignment concretely links to her classmates and teacher (her school network), her parents (her family network) and her friends at home (her outside of school network). All three networks have particular expectations of Leah that impact her continuous identity element production.

Some Analytical Capabilities

1   Discovery of how the continuous identity element is produced in line with a particular network.
2   Discovery of how continuous identity element production can impact the belonging (or not belonging) to particular networks.

Networks with their unwritten laws and regulations, mediating forms and tight to loose connections produce the identity of a social actor in an intermediary sense.

(Norris 2011: 187)

Continuous identity elements are those identity elements that concretely link to a social actor's network(s). A social actor produces themselves in a particular way, constructing a specific identity element. The network learns how the social actor produces themselves as having that specific identity element and in turn enforces that identity element back upon the social actor as a continuous identity element. As an example, we now revisit the example of Leah writing an essay for her history class.

As Leah writes her essay for her high school history class, she not only produces an immediate student identity element, she also produces a continuous student identity element. While the immediate student identity element is produced through her performance of her higher-level mediated action of actually doing the assignment, her continuous student identity element is produced in connection with her networks: classmates and teacher, parents and friends outside of school. Let us assume that Leah's classmates and her teacher value education. Her parents, however, do not value education very highly and neither do her friends outside of school.

In the beginning when Leah started school, we would have found that Leah's continuous identity element as a student (superimposed over her immediate identity element) was conflicted due to her networks placing different pressures on her. Leah's classmates and teacher network wanted Leah to do well in school and they expected her to finish her assignments. Whereas, Leah's parents and her friends at home, who saw education as less valuable, would have rather seen Leah do other things than studying or writing essays. Leah in turn had to respond to the various pressures, producing a continuous student identity element that was viable in relation to her networks.

Now, let us imagine that Leah continuously produced a good student identity element. This continuous identity element was (in time) taken up as Leah's continuous student identity element and then became reinforced by all of her networks. If Leah at some point in time would now decide not to do her assignment, a social actor from her family or outside of school network would likely comment by saying something as "and I always thought you were a good student." Thus, while networks exert pressure upon a social actor, the social actor has the option to align more with one network than with another. Certainly, many other possibilities exist, but the important point is that the networks, even when not aligned with (here Leah's parents and friends at home), will create new pressures that will hold the social actor (Leah) to the alignment that she chose (her school network), reinforcing her continuous good student identity element.

Thus, this identity element is called continuous, since it has to be continuously produced in some way so that it is acceptably linked to the social actor's networks. Because of this, once established, a continuous identity element is not easily changed.

General Identity Element Production

History

Developed in Norris (2002), first published in Norris (2011).

Theory

Social actors produce concrete higher-level mediated actions, producing identity elements. These concretely performed higher-level mediated actions with their produced identity elements are connected to concrete institutions, extended networks and parts of society. These linkages to concrete institutions, concrete extensive networks and concrete parts of society build an outer layer of discourse. The outer layer of discourse can relatively strongly constrain the social actor's agency.

Analytical Tool

The general identity is an analytical tool that showcases how concretely performed higher-level mediated actions and the produced identity elements are linked to and (often quite strongly) constrained by concrete institutions, extended networks and parts of society. Again, we can find discrepancies between various institutions, extended networks and parts of society that concretely link to the higher-level mediated actions and identity elements that a social actor produces.

Example

Leah writes an essay for her high school history class. Leah's writing of her assignment concretely links to her school institution and the immediate and wider institution of family. Both of these institutions have particular expectations on Leah that impact her general identity element production.

Some Analytical Capabilities

1 Discovery of how the general identity element is produced in line with particular institutions.
2 Discovery of how the general identity element can be constrained by particular institutions.

General identities are constructed through actions and produced through the practices in the social-time-place that the social actor inhabits, all of which concern the identity elements by and large.

(Norris 2011: 181)

General identity elements are those identity elements that are created through the social actor's concrete links with institutions and aspects of society. Outer layer discourses and thus general identity elements are often prescribed to social actors by the institutions. As long as a social actor has internalized the prescribed identity elements, the outer layer discourses are invisible. Outer layer discourses only become clearly visible when a tension between the various levels of discourse exists.

In our example of Leah writing her history essay, the institutional outer layer school discourse is invisible because she adheres to what the institution school expects of her. She also adheres to what the institutional outer layer family discourse expects of her (in order to differentiate between Leah's family network and the institution of family, we can for example think of the Parent–Teacher Association). Both the institution family values a good student, as does the institution school.

However, when outer layer discourses produce vastly different general identity elements than the social actor produces on the immediate and the continuous level, this can lead to great strain for the social actor and can lead to mental illness. See Norris (2011) for a case-study of conflicting outer layer discourses prescribing different general identity elements to a social actor and Norris and Matelau-Doherty (forthcoming) for further discussion on this topic.

The Coming Together of Three Concrete Layers of an Identity Element

History

Developed in Norris (2002), first published in Norris (2011).

Theory

Social actors produce concrete higher-level mediated actions, producing identity elements. These concrete higher-level mediated actions with their identity elements build the social actor's central layer of discourse. In this central layer of discourse, the social actor's agency is relatively high. Simultaneously, the higher-level mediated actions and produced identity elements are concretely linked to the social actor's network(s). With this concrete network-link, the higher-level mediated actions produce continuous identity elements at the intermediary layer of discourse. The intermediary layer of discourse constrains the social actor's agency to some extent. Again, simultaneously both of these—the concretely performed mediated actions with their produced identity elements and the continuous linkages to specific networks—are connected to concrete institutions, extended networks and parts of the society. With these linkages to concrete institutions, concrete extensive networks and concrete parts of society, the higher-level mediated actions with their produced identity elements build a general identity element at the outer layer of discourse. The outer layer of discourse is a concrete layer that the social actor is connected to but one which can relatively strongly constrain the social actor's agency.

Analytical Tool

Vertical identity production is an analytical tool that brings together three concrete layers of discourse: the central or action level, the intermediary or network level and the outer or institutional level of discourse.

With this analytical tool, we can analyze how a social actor first creates an immediate identity element by performing a concrete higher-level mediated action; how the social actor, second, creates a continuous identity element as the concretely performed higher-level mediated action links to particular networks; and how the social actor, third, creates a general identity element as the concretely performed higher-level mediated action links to particular institutions.

One concretely produced higher-level mediated action and immediate identity element can be accepted by one concrete network, building a continuous identity element, but may also be rejected by another concrete network. Thus, we may find incongruity in the intermediary layer of discourse. Similarly, the concrete mediated action and identity element performed is (often quite strongly) constrained by concrete institutions, extended networks and parts of society, which concretely link to the higher-level mediated action and identity element produced. Again, we can find discrepancies between various institutions, extended networks and parts of society that link to the higher-level mediated action and produced identity element.

A concretely performed higher-level mediated action and identity element that displays congruence on all layers of (concrete) discourse is an action and identity element that adheres to social norms on all three of these levels of discourse.[2]

Example

Leah writes an essay for her high school history class. As Leah writes her assignment, she produces her immediate student identity element.

Leah's writing of her assignment concretely links to her classmates and teacher (her school network), her parents (her family network) and her friends at home (her outside of school network). All three networks have particular expectations of Leah that impact her continuous identity element production.

Leah's writing of her assignment concretely links to her institutions of school and family. Both of these institutions have particular expectations of Leah that impact her general identity element production.

Some Analytical Capabilities

1   Discovery of how concretely performed mediated actions and their produced identity elements are a part of different layers of (concrete) discourse with different constraints.
2   Discovery of how some concretely performed higher-level mediated actions and the produced identity elements are congruent on all levels, while other concrete higher-level mediated actions and produced identity elements are disparate at the intermediary or outer layer of discourse or both.
3   Discovery of how agency is affected in and by the various layers of discourse and how social actors navigate these different constraints.

The analytical tool of vertical identity allows us to delineate various layers of discourse that produce an immediate, continuous and general identity element. Often (but not always), all three layers of identity elements are produced simultaneously. See Norris (2011) for a case-study example where only general identity elements were being produced.

Often, the outer layer discourses and the resulting general identity elements are prescribed so that social actors have little influence on them. However, see Christensson (2018) and Matelau-Doherty (forthcoming) for research studies in which social actors actively drew on or changed the outer layer discourses to produce (concrete) general identity elements.

Intermediary layers of discourse and the resulting continuous identity elements may initially be more agentively produced by social actors, but once the networks are aware of the identity elements, the networks enforce them. Therefore, continuous identity elements become difficult to change.

Concrete layers of discourse and the resulting immediate identity elements are the ones that social actors have most agency over, but here, of course practices and larger (often ephemeral) societal discourses (mediated actions with a history and mediated actions with a history with an institutional dimension which are not concretely linked to the social actor) often play a normative role.

Site of Engagement

History

Developed in Scollon (1998), refined in Norris and Jones (2005), used in relation to identity in Norris (2011), and further refined in Norris (2014b, 2019).

Theory

Every concretely performed higher-level mediated action that builds a concrete identity element is performed at a site of engagement, which makes the production of the higher-level mediated action and its identity element possible by linking to at least one (but often more) practice(s) as well as to at least one (but often more) societal discourse(s). Concrete immediate, continuous and general identity elements thus come together with practices and larger societal discourses at a site of engagement. Practices are defined as higher-level mediated actions with a history (Scollon 1998) and discourses are defined as higher-level mediated actions with a history (practices) with an institutional dimension (Norris 2014b). Both practices and larger societal discourses prescribe identity elements to social actors.

Analytical Tool

When a social actor produces a concrete higher-level mediated action and with it produces an identity element, this action links to the abstracted level (practice), which incorporates all of those previously (often by other social actors) performed higher-level mediated actions (actions with a history, i.e., practices). Simultaneously, the (concrete) higher-level mediated action and identity element links to societal discourses (those practices that have an institutional dimension). Often, we find that some practices and/or discourses converge with the concrete higher-level mediated action and its produced identity element, whereas at other times, we find that some practices and/or discourses diverge from the concretely performed higher-level mediated action and produced identity element.

Examples

Ben and Zoe have a three-month-old baby. Ben has taken on the role of stay-at-home dad, while Zoe is working.

Within the site of engagement, all concrete layers of discourse, the central, intermediary and outer layers of discourse, are produced and come together with practices and larger societal discourses.

In this example, Ben produces an immediate father identity element on the concrete central layer of discourse; and Zoe produces an immediate mother identity element on the concrete central layer of discourse. On the concrete intermediary level of discourse (linking to their networks), both parents produce continuous father and mother identity elements that show Ben as the primary caregiver and Zoe as the breadwinner. On the concrete outer layer of discourse, Ben is produced as a minority primary caregiver (as he is interacting with many mothers who take up this role and few fathers), while Zoe's identity element as the working mother is produced.

These concrete layers of discourse and the identity production intersect at the site of engagement with multiple practices such as the practice of mothering (notice that we do not have a comparable word for a father such as fathering), the practice of caregiving and so on. Practices are the ways that things are done in Ben's and Zoe's society. They may live in a society where sharing responsibility and taking turns at primary caregiving is the norm, or they may live in a society where such parental constellation is still unusual. These normative practices prescribe identity elements. While that does not mean that the social actor *has to abide* by the norms, it does mean that the social actor is continuously confronted by these practices and by the prescribed identity elements. When examining the practice level, we find how parenting is expected to be done and which identity elements are prescribed to the parents that they either take up (making the practices quite invisible) or challenge (making the practices clearly visible), and eventually producing a change in the practices.

Besides the practice level of how things are done and what that means for identity element production, we find larger societal discourses about parenting. These can be found in the media, on social networking sites, in pamphlets (for example in some societies, predominantly mothers may be depicted when it comes to primary caregiving topics), and so on. These larger societal discourses again prescribe identity elements to the social actors. Again, this does not mean that the social actors have to abide by them, but it does mean that they are continuously confronted by these larger societal discourses and prescribed identity elements. When examining the larger discourse level, we find how parenting is expected to be done and which identity elements are prescribed to the parents that they either take up (making the societal discourses quite invisible) or challenge (making the societal discourses clearly visible), and eventually producing a change in the societal discourses.

Some Analytical Capabilities

1. Discovery of how a concrete higher-level mediated action and the produced identity element are shaped by converging and/or diverging practices.
2. Discovery of how a concrete higher-level mediated action and the produced identity element are shaped by converging and/or diverging societal discourses.
3. Discovery of how many practices and how many societal discourses are at play when a particular higher-level mediated action and identity element are being produced.
4. Discovery of how practices and societal discourses enforce a certain higher-level mediated action and identity element.
5. Discovery of how practices and societal discourses are being shaped and changed by concrete contestations of identity elements through the production of specific higher-level mediated actions.

The site of engagement is that window opened up through practices and discourses that make the concrete higher-level mediated action possible (Scollon 1998; Norris 2014b). Since every mediated action also produces identity (Scollon 1997), and identity can be teased apart on the concrete micro level into an immediate, continuous and general identity element (which often, but not always come about simultaneously), the site of engagement is the coming together of all concrete levels of identity with practices and larger societal discourses. The site of engagement thus forces the analyst to bring in the meso (practice) level and the macro (societal discourse) level. Thus, the concept of a site of engagement makes clear that we can never just get stuck at one level, be that the micro (concrete higher-level mediated action with its various layers of concrete discourses and identity element formations), the meso (practice) or the macro (societal discourse) level.

When we take the example above, we can draw a diagram that illustrates how the concrete higher-level mediated actions of Ben caring for the baby as a stay-at-home father and Zoe going to work at one moment in time are impacted by practices and discourses (Figure 3.5).

Here, at this site of engagement, as he is staying home with the baby, Ben produces a primary caregiver identity element on all concrete levels. As Zoe is leaving for work, her higher-level mediated action produces a working mother identity element on all concrete levels. Their identity element production is simultaneously impacted by the practice of mothering, the practice of father as primary breadwinner, the practice of sharing parental responsibility to name a few. Simultaneously,

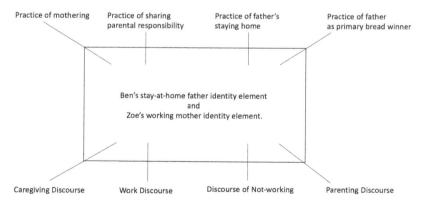

Figure 3.5 Site of engagement of Ben staying at home with the baby while Zoe is leaving for work.

the site of engagement is intersected by larger societal discourses such as the parenting discourse, the caregiving discourse, the work discourse, the discourse of not working and so on.

Scales of Action

History

First published in Norris (2009b), clearly developed as analytical tool with a link to identity in Norris (2017b).

Theory

Social actors continuously produce consecutive actions, all of which produce identity elements. However, not all consecutive actions and their identity elements are linked. While small scale higher-level mediated actions and their produced identity elements are always embedded in larger scale higher-level mediated actions forming a larger scale identity element, they do not necessarily belong to the same larger scale higher-level mediated action and identity element even if performed quickly in succession. For example, a social actor can perform five consecutive higher-level mediated actions within a relatively short time, all of which produce identity elements. Three of the higher-level mediated actions and their produced identity elements belong together and these three combined build a larger scale higher-level mediated action and identity element, while the other two higher-level mediated actions and their produced identity elements belong to sets of completely different higher-level mediated actions and identity elements, each building their own larger scale higher-level mediated actions and larger scale identity elements.

Analytical Tool

When a social actor performs a higher-level mediated action producing an identity element, this action and identity element are often linked to other higher-level mediated actions and produced identity elements. Higher-level mediated actions and the identity elements that are produced can be teased apart to be of a smaller or larger scale. The analyst first teases apart various higher-level mediated actions and their produced identity elements and analyzes their various scales and how they are embedded, and then determines to which larger scale higher-level mediated actions and larger scale identity elements they belong.

Example

Karen, who has a catering business, goes shopping for groceries with her children and then helps them with homework.

Karen makes a shopping list.
Karen drives to the supermarket.
Karen speaks with the children about homework.
Karen buys groceries.
Karen drives home.
Karen speaks with the children about homework.
Karen unpacks the car.
Karen puts the groceries away.
Karen helps the children with their homework.

Here, we find two larger scale higher-level mediated actions and their identity elements: (1) shopping for groceries (let us imagine Karen has to drive to the store) and the identity element of a caterer and (2) helping with homework and the identity element of a mother.

While the higher-level mediated actions of speaking with the children about homework and Karen's mother identity element are clearly embedded in the higher-level mediated action of driving, the actual larger scale higher-level action is of a different kind than shopping for groceries of which the two drives are an intricate part and which produce Karen's caterer identity element. In fact, when thinking about which identity element a higher-level mediated action produces, it is often quite easy to tease the various consecutively performed higher-level mediated actions apart. This also easily allows for the analysis of which larger scale higher-level mediated actions and identity elements they belong to.

Some Analytical Capabilities

1   Discovery of how social actors perform higher-level mediated actions and identity elements that are part of different larger scale higher-level mediated actions and identity elements produced consecutively.

2   Discovery of how other social actors understand the performed higher-level mediated actions and identity elements as clearly belonging to different larger scale higher-level mediated actions and larger scale identity elements.

3   Discovery that social actors can produce simultaneous higher-level mediated actions and identity elements belonging to different larger scale higher-level actions and larger scale identity elements.

Scales of action is a tool that allows us to analyze which identity elements a social actor produces consecutively and/or simultaneously in time that link to various larger scale identity elements. We may find that a social actor produces particular identity elements together with other particular identity elements, while the social actor may in fact never produce again different identity elements with either of those, either directly consecutively or simultaneously, making a larger scale identity element distinct.

Examining how identity elements and their larger scale identity elements are produced over time gives us a deeper understanding of a social actor's identity production. Scales of action can be a particularly valuable tool when analyzing identity change and/or the stabilization of identity (for change of identity and stabilization of identity, see Norris 2011).

Conclusion

This chapter has outlined the history and theory of 16 analytical tools and their analytical capabilities for the analysis of human identity production in action and interaction. By giving examples and drawing connections between the analytical concepts, the chapter demonstrates how the analytical tools comprehensively fit together, building a cohesive theory and methodology.

Rather than simplifying the complexity of identity production in (inter)action by focusing on either the micro level *or* the meso (practice) level *or* the macro (societal discourse) level, the framework, with its multiple strongly theoretically grounded analytical tools, allows for the systematic analysis of the complexity that is found in everyday identity production through action and interaction. With this possibility of analyzing the inherent complexity in everyday identity, we can begin to draw strong connections between the three concrete micro levels of identity production in actions and interactions, the meso practice level and the macro societal discourse level. The ability to analyze the various levels based on one theoretical/ analytical framework allows us to shed new insight onto identity production.

Notes

1 For details about multimodal transcription conventions, see Chapter 2 and Norris (2004a, 2011, or 2019).
2 This is only one aspect of normativity that can be analyzed. Another can be found below in the section on practice.

References

Christensson, J. 2018. 'This is where my inner history teacher appears': A methodological approach to analysing student teachers' professional identity in interaction. *Classroom Discourse* 10(2), 168–187. doi: 10.1080/19463014.2018.1530685.

Norris, S. 2002. A theoretical framework for multimodal discourse analysis presented via the analysis of identity construction of two women living in Germany. Department of Linguistics: Georgetown University. Dissertation: UMI.

Norris, S. 2004a. *Analyzing multimodal interaction: A methodological framework*. London: Routledge.

Norris, S. 2004b. Multimodal discourse analysis: A conceptual framework. In: Levine, P. and Scollon, R. (eds.) *Discourse and technology: Multimodal discourse analysis*. Washington, DC: Georgetown University Press, 101–115.

Norris, S. 2005. Habitus, social identity, the perception of male domination – And agency? In: Norris, Sigrid and Jones, R. (eds.) *Discourse in action: Introducing mediated discourse analysis*. London: Routledge, 183–197.

Norris, S. 2007. The micropolitics of personal national and ethnicity identity. *Discourse and Society* 18(5), 653–674.

Norris, S. 2008. Some thoughts on personal identity construction: A multimodal perspective. In: Bhatia, Vijay, Flowerdew, John, and Jones, Rodney H. (eds.) *New directions in discourse*. London: Routledge, 132–149.

Norris, S. 2009a. Modal density and modal configurations: Multimodal actions. In Jewit, C. (ed.) *Routledge handbook for multimodal discourse analysis*. London: Routledge.

Norris, S. 2009b. Tempo, *Auftakt*, Levels of actions, and practice: Rhythms in ordinary interactions. *Journal of Applied Linguistics* 6(3), 333–356.

Norris, S. 2011. *Identity in (inter)action: Introducing multimodal (inter)action analysis*. Berlin and Boston, MA: deGruyter Mouton.

Norris, S. 2013. What is a mode? Smell, olfactory perception, and the notion of mode in multimodal mediated theory. *Multimodal Communication* 2(2), 155–169.

Norris, S. 2014a. Learning tacit classroom participation. WCLTA. *Procedia Social and Behavioral Sciences* 141, 166–170. Elsevier.

Norris, S. 2014b. The impact of literacy based schooling on learning a creative practice: Modal configurations, practices and discourses. *Multimodal Communication* 3(2), 181–195.

Norris, S. and Makboon, B. 2015. Objects, Frozen actions, and identity: A multimodal (inter)action analysis. *Multimodal Communication* 4(1), 43–60.

Norris, S. 2017a. Rhythmus und Resonanz in internationalen Videokonferenzen. In: Breyer, T., Buchholz, M., Hamburger, A., and Pfänder S. (eds.). *Resonanz, Rhythmus & Synchronisierung: Erscheinungsformen und Effekte*. Bielefeld: transcript-Verlag.

Norris, S. 2017b. Scales of action: An example of driving & car talk in Germany and North America. *Text & Talk* 37(1), 117–139.

Norris, S. 2019. *Systematically working with multimodal data: Research methods in multimodal discourse analysis*. Hoboken, NJ: Wiley Blackwell.

Norris, S. and Jones, R.H. 2005. *Discourse in action: Introducing mediated discourse analysis*. London: Routledge.

Scollon, R. 1997. Handbills, tissues, and condoms: A site of engagement for the construction of identity in public discourse. *Journal of Sociolinguistics* 1(1), 39–61.

Scollon, R. 1998. *Mediated discourse as social interaction: A study of news discourse*. London: Longman.

Scollon, R. 2001. *Mediated discourse: The nexus of practice*. London: Routledge.

Vygotsky, L.S. 1978. *Mind in society: The development of higher psychological processes*, eds. M. Cole, V. John-Steiner, S. Scribner, and E. Souberman. Cambridge, MA: Harvard University Press.

Wertsch, J.V. 1998. *Voices of the mind: A sociocultural approach to mediated action*. Cambridge, MA: Harvard University Press.

Index